fEB . 67

Snapshots of Vietnam

The Unraveling of a Non-Combatant

James F.P. Marsh

Temenos Publishing Company

© Copyright 2010 James F.P. Marsh

Cover art by Mitchell Crisp

ISBN 978-0-9785648-0-3

Temenos Publishing Company
411 Main St.
Argenta Arts District
North Little Rock, AR 72114
501-772-7602
www.temcnospublishing.com

For my wife Anita Sue Marsh, whose heart steers with perseverance and courage. For our four children, Susan, Mary, Andrea, and Peter, and their uniqueness. For the late Captain Richard E. Mayo, 15th Combat Engineers, whose leadership kept our company in line. For the late Sergeant Johnnie Jones and his courage. For all the men of B-Company, 4th/47th Infantry. And for Gary Bayles, Fred Silkey, Robert Bayly, and all fellow soldiers.

Table of Contents

Detaching from the Spool

Unraveling

Exposed

Processing

Postscript

Acknowledgements

Paula Morell, my editor, is like a weaver sitting at a loom, taking overlooked or discarded threads and turning out tapestries called books. People like Paula have been placed in my life like stepping stones along a bumpy, winding road. They've allowed me to stand on their shoulders in order to see my way.

Others are not mentioned in this book, but they are no less important: Bernard P. Gerrity of Mahopac, New York; if not for him, I wouldn't be alive today; I pay respect to the late Dr. Bill Bright for his "little blue book" which helps me even to this day; I owe a debt of gratitude to the Institute in Basic Life Principles; thanks to Dr. Charles R. Solomon of Pigeon Forge, Tennessee, for tirelessly teaching truth; my hat comes off for the late Jack H. Wilson—thanks for pouring his cement-like convictions into my life for thirty-one years.

I wish you could meet Damon B. Walker of Belleview, Florida; Mickey Evans of Dunklin Memorial Camp, Okeechobee, Florida, and Retired Air Force Chaplain John Meyer, all giants among men.

Foreword

Have you ever heard an Air Ambulance helicopter fly overhead and have it bring back images of med evacs with bodies of young men in bags being off loaded? This is what happens to me occasionally of my tour in Vietnam.

In *Snapshots of Vietnam*, James F. Marsh captures pictures that need to be shared. Those of us who served in Vietnam have often hidden those all too painful experiences. Jim's honest descriptions will stir up reminders for the reader. He's captured the heart of what one carries away from war: some good, others bad, some serious, others humorous.

What is important is that the author has been able to overcome the bad memories. He shows that all of us need something to bring us through dangerous times of life, and still are able to live full and complete lives today. Read this story of a young man who deals with life as it came to him in Vietnam, and then how he dealt with the impact on his life.

—Guenther (Jerry) Horn, Lt Col USAF (Ret)

Preface

Writing a book about my thirteen months in Vietnam and the years that followed was the furthest thing from my mind in 2004. Then a gray-haired woman walked up to me at a *Cedars of Lebanon* conference in Texas, changing my life forever.

Through her tears she said, "My son was a Vietnam vet. He committed suicide. He felt guilty that he survived."

We hugged, and she cried on my shoulder.

Later I thought, *Suppose her son had read something that might have helped him?*

Three years later my fingers tremble as I punch Gary Bayles' phone numbers into my cell. Forty years. *Would he remember me?*

"Hello?"

"Is this Gary Bayles who was in Vietnam?"

"Yes."

"This is Jim Marsh. I don't know if you remember me—"

"Marsh! Well, how are you doing? It's good to hear from you."

We spend fifteen minutes catching up on four decades. I tell him about the book I'm writing.

"Hey Bayles, you got any pictures?"

"I've got a box—" There is a pause, just enough to make me uncomfortable. "I've got a camera in the closet. Still has film in it. I never did develop it. It's still hanging there."

It is for these, and the thousands of others, that I write.

—James F. P. Marsh

Tightly Wound

I'm Gone

"You've got a letter," my mother says, twisting her apron strings. "It's from the government." She scans my face like a physician looking for symptoms as I tear open the envelope with an official seal.

Greetings, from Uncle Sam. You are being drafted.

I glance at the stained calendar on the green wall. Friday, December 31st, 1965, just three days after I left my teens. My blood ices like the weather outside. Mom's eyes search mine.

"Happy New Year, Mom," I say, and hand her the letter.

She clutches it to her breast, then hands it back. She moves into the kitchen. As Mom faces the sink, she turns on the water to muffle her sobs. She is fifty-five and I am her baby.

"I'm going to borrow the car," I say, and lay the letter next to me on the seat. The 1959 Chrysler aims toward White Plains on 287. Will I run?

I drive the speed limit and roll down the windows inviting in the gray cold. I think back three years. It was the night before a high school football game and I had tried to catch pneumonia. My plan was to open the bathroom window after a cold shower and stand naked, inviting the quarter-sized snowflakes to blow in sideways to hit my chest. I envisioned lying in the hospital bed, excused from playing left halfback and safety. It didn't work then, and I know it won't now.

From White Plains I head north, rolling into a quaint town named Carmel. I park in front of an open church resembling something out of "Little House on the Prairie." The sanctuary is like a warm womb. Candles flicker. I touch the ancient oak pews and take in the aroma of incense. *Sanctuary.*

I spread the letter on the wooden altar rail and kneel, listening to myself breathe.

"Lord, I don't know what to do. Show me," I whisper aloud. I wait. One minute, five minutes, more.

Finally it comes. *Do what they tell you.*

I rise and drive home.

Mom greets me with piercing eyes, like an FBI agent looking for evidence, scrutinizing my face for clues.

"I'm going in the Army. I'll do what they tell me."

I am the last of her five children.

She turns like a wax figure on a slow swivel and staggers to the kitchen, tugging her apron strings. With her back to me, she twists the tap and lowers her head, shoulders shaking.

The Marines Are Drafting

Standing in single file in my boxer shorts at the Whitehall Street Induction Center isn't my idea of Christmas season fun. I can feel the tiny drops of perspiration forming in my armpits. No one is smiling except a wiry fellow near the front.

He keeps turning around laughing. His dark, wavy hair is combed like Buddy Holly. His antics amuse me, and I am calmed by his happy countenance.

Without warning a massive, crusty sergeant enters shouting, "Who wants to join the Marines?"

Two fellows behind me say, "We're from Harrison. We'll go." They jump out of line and hustle to the front.

"That's two," the giant says. "Are there any more?"

I glance to the front at the smiling guy. He doesn't move.

Two more young men shout, "We're from the Bronx; we'll go."

The sweat rolls to the band of my shorts.

Finally, the Marine barks, "Ok, I'm going to pick every fifth one."

I panic. He yanks the smiling guy out of line first. I lean to my left and do the fastest count imaginable. I would be a fifth.

I bolt out of line and run to the back. The Marine pulls out the kid who had stood behind me and ushers him to the front. He turns and looks me in the eye, as if to say, "How could you do such a thing?"

Smiley stands with them, his countenance unchanged.

Scoop Gallello

Scoop is the only guy I can look down to. I'm five-four. He must be five-three. I loved hanging around him at parties and on the Avenue back home. He has a low hairline and resembles a Mafia bodyguard. His muscular arms hang lower than average.

On January 11, 1966, we raise our right hands to swear in. All, that is, except Scoop. He raises his left hand.

The officer facing us screams, "What's the matter with you, boy? Raise your right hand like I am!"

Scoop still has his left up and says, "I'm doing the same side you are."

The officer sighs. "Repeat after me."

Scoop turns and whispers, "Everybody, cross your fingers."

We all cross them on the left hand. All except Scoop. He crosses his right.

In basic training at Fort Jackson, South Carolina, we love the P.T. Test. One of the five events is to swing from rung to rung on an overhead ladder without dropping off. We all try for one hundred points, or eighty-nine rungs.

I get my eighty-nine and say, "My hands won't open up. My forearms are locked."

Scoop gets his hundred points. "That was easy," he says.

One of his buddies says, "I can't do this. Will you do the rungs for me?"

Scoop says, "Sure. Change shirts so they'll see your nametag on me."

Scoop does another eighty-nine rungs. I double over with laughter. "How do you do that?" I ask.

He ignores my question, as if there is no explanation.

"Does anybody else need to qualify?" he asks the group.

Basic Training Done

John Boraski fidgets in his seat next to me, staring out of the small window of the DC-7 destined for New York.

"It'll be good to see the neighborhood again," he says.

"I'm just glad to be done with Basic."

"Yeah." John's cobalt eyes match the cloudless March sky. His high cheekbones, his blond hair—that Elvis hair now buzzed—and sheepish half-grin give him that kid-next-door look.

"John, the expert rifleman," I tease. "Nice trophy."

"How about you," he shoots back, "with your plaque for the Fitness Test?" Then John turns to me with a twinkle and whispers, "I stole a hand grenade."

"You WHAT?"

"I took a grenade from the company supply room."

"Are you nuts?" I scan his dress greens for a bulge. "Where is it?"

"It's in my duffle bag."

I lean back and sigh, fumbling with the complimentary bag of peanuts. My hand shakes as I try to sip the Coke. I imagine us spiraling into the Atlantic after an explosion in the baggage section. *Great. I survive Basic only to be stranded at sea, bobbing like a buoy off Jones Beach.*

I watch the stewardess moving her blue jacketed arms like playing charades. "In the event of a sudden change in cabin pressure, the compartment above will open." I raise my eyes to the place where the oxygen tubing will drop, then run my hand over the seat that will become my floating device.

Boraski gazes out the window, still smiling.

Soon the captain announces, "We're approaching Kennedy Airport." The plane banks hard to the left. Below, the dark Atlantic glistens with whitecaps dancing in the sun.

Boraski leans over and says, "Did you hear about the plane crash here last month where the wing hit the water? They said it did a cartwheel and crashed. Everybody died."

"No, I didn't," I say, craning to estimate our altitude. "It does look close."

John unbuckles his seatbelt, stands and begins shouting, "We're going to crash! The wing is going to hit the water!"

Heads turn, wide-eyed. People fumble with carry-ons and yank at purses. Miss Bluejacket rushes to Row J and earns her pay trying to calm him. "Sir," she says, "Sit down!"

John keeps shouting, "Pull up! Pull up!"

"Sir, sit down NOW!"

I can feel the perspiration on my upper lip when we taxi to the terminal. John flashes me a coy smile.

I have this uneasy feeling as we all watch for the unloaded bags on the spinning conveyance.

John smiles again as he lifts his duffle bag.

Unit Training at Fort Riley

George Washington Schook stands in front of the field class on demolition at Ft. Riley, Kansas. It's a sweltering day in July, 1966. His stubby, sausage-like fingers mold the white C-4 plastic explosive like a sculptor, fashioning his artwork for our combat engineer platoon.

Schook's gravel voice doesn't need a microphone. "To make a cratering charge," he says, "you press the bottom into a concave shape."

In front of me sits Andrew Vito, a short muscular fireplug from Brooklyn. Vito turns and whispers, "I like this guy," giving his Imprimatur on the Sarge. We heard Schook had been in the Korean War, so he already has our respect.

Schook's broad shoulders and barrel chest make him look as if he always holds his breath. His massive arms hang in curves around his bulging mid-section. They don't swing when he walks. Every other sentence is punctuated by dry, white spit, not carefully aimed. With a toothless smile he delivers instructions with the finesse of a college professor. "You form the nosecone the same way, only pointing it upward."

Day after day he preaches safety first. When he warns of booby-traps, he says, "Never take chances. Blow them in place. If anyone wants a souvenir, tell him to give you five minutes to walk away. Safety is the key." All heads nod. Even the talkative Vito falls silent.

One weekend, Vito gets Schook to take him to town for a tattoo. That evening Vito pulls back his sleeve to show off his "Mom and Dad" hearts. "Sergeant Schook took me to get it," he says.

It is the talk of the company.

Phillip MacIntosh

Phil MacIntosh of Parma, Ohio has a voice like a megaphone. A natural storyteller, Mac belts a banshee "Whoooh!" every chance he gets. "I sat in the barber chair at the Induction Center," he says. "When those clippers ran roads across my head and beard, I said, Whoooh!"

At Ft. Riley, a tornado warning comes over. Captain Mayo says, "Open the windows and get on your bunks." We all obey. The roof feels like it's coming off. I hear nails squeak, pried from the wood. Upstairs Mac begins hollering his familiar, "Whoooh!" A sucking sensation lifts us all about two inches from the mattress. Phil keeps yelling till it eases us down.

MacIntosh dramatizes driving his souped-up '55 Chevy. He'd warn the children on his street, "Now when you see or hear me coming, you'd better get out of the way cause you'll get run over." He says, "I come down my block fifty miles an hour. Whoooh!"

Phil has one drawback though, and that's his mouth. Swear words highlight every sentence. One day some guys secretly record his conversation. They place the recorder on his bunk and play it back. He asks, "Who is that SOB?"

They say, "It's you."

He plays it through twice, eyebrows lowered; he's shaking his head. He vows to never cuss again. That's MacIntosh, all or nothing; entertaining, loveable, confrontational, and fearless.

Our platoon is sent a man named Shifley. Somehow Mac finds out that he is a thief. The judge tells Shifley, "Army or prison, you choose."

Mac says, "Shifley, you're shiftless. Watch this guy."

Every day, "Watch him, he's Shiftless. What did you steal today?"

Shiftless disappears a week before we leave for Asia.

Flatcars

President Lyndon B. Johnson flexes his muscles, enduing all power to Robert McNamara. If a young man quits college, the draft machines scoop him up like front end loaders at a landfill. Many draftees make up the Ninth Infantry Division.

We are the 15th Combat Engineers with a glorious past that lay dormant since World War II. We fought through North Africa, the Beaches of England, and into France. Now we are awakened. Our battalion will be the advance party, early birds to Southeast Asia.

Our beloved Sergeant D'Armitt says, "Take these three-pound hammers and bags of nails. Fix the chocks behind every wheel."

Bobby Cutro, Fred Silkey, and I look down the long railroad track. "Where's the end of this thing?" Bobby asks. The loading docks at Ft. Riley are like the queen bee's quarters in the military hive. With hammers swinging, we secure trucks, jeeps, and tanks on the flatbed train cars.

After three days, Bobby says, "My forearm feels like Popeye's."

"Mine feels like Bluto's," I say, prying my fingers from the handle.

Bobby grew up in Jersey City and had a minimum wage job as a runner on Wall Street. He smiles, "At the end of every day I'd pick up paper off the floor."

Whenever Bobby is around, laughter rings out like a contagious bug. He must have been weaned on Dale Carnegie's *How to Win Friends and Influence People.*

Fred Silkey hails from Granby, Connecticut. He smokes a pipe. Kind of like the fellow you'd see in a plaid shirt and khakis sitting by a fireplace with a Golden Retriever at his feet.

In a few days we will board the train on our first leg of the Asian journey.

Classified Info

Top Sergeant looks over the company in formation at Ft. Riley and announces, "We're going to Asia."

"But what country?" we all ask.

"We can't tell you," he says. "Secret. Classified."

Two weeks earlier I stood in my mom's kitchen, stirring a pot of underwear. I poured in the olive drab dye. "Ma, we could be going to Thailand," I said. "Maybe Vietnam, I don't know for sure. They won't tell us."

"Why not?" she asked, then twisted her apron strings.

"I don't know. It's like some clandestine operation."

At last, on September 29, 1966, our unit leaves Ft. Riley to ride the train to California. There we board the USS Sultan in San Francisco. I feel like Samson entering the Philistine prison. Five thousand troops squeeze into tight quarters. The bunks are stacked five-high. I make sure I don't get under the two hundred pound Seigford.

"One thing I know," MacIntosh says as we sail under the Golden Gate, "we ain't going to Germany."

"Yeah. Maybe Korea. That's Asia."

Ten days out, halfway across the Pacific, a helicopter hovers, dropping mailbags.

MacIntosh receives a *TIME Magazine* along with his letters. He opens to a feature story. "Hey! Look at this."

We gather around, peering over his shoulder. The story's title is "Ninth Infantry Division." It shows a map of the Mekong Delta in Vietnam. Red arrows all point up the rivers from the South China Sea.

"Hey, Sarge," Mac says, "do you think the enemy gets *TIME Magazine*?"

The Viet Cong know we're coming.

Message on a Tin Can

Francisco "Pancho" Martinez and I lean on the rail of the USS Sultan staring at the flying fish as they glide between the green swells. The brisk October wind bites through our fatigues as we ponder our fate. A week ago we watched the Golden Gate sink on the horizon to our rear.

"Do you think we'll make it back?"

His question doesn't elicit an immediate answer. Pancho is the tough-acting Chicano from L.A. He plays the Low Rider image, homemade tattoos on his hands. At night he wears a black silk stocking on his head. "Your hair should never go forward," he says.

He teases Kenny Fraiman from Brooklyn to no end. Pancho the comic.

But not today.

I glance at him and think I see a tear. I look back to the sea. "Pancho, I believe I'll make it back."

"I hope I do," he says, and lowers his head.

Now and then a porpoise jumps. No land in any direction. We're bobbing like a bottle with a message inside. *Help! We're twenty and being sent to war.*

Out of the corner of my eye, I see the tear trickling down his cheek.

"I'm praying every minute," I say.

"Yeah." His voice quivers.

On that cloudless afternoon somewhere in the middle of the Pacific, on the deck of a rolling troop ship crammed with five thousand soldiers, Pancho is scared to death.

"God takes care of the flying fish," I say. "He'll take care of us."

"Yeah," he says, hiding his head in his arms.

McGee

After twenty days at sea, our first stop is to refuel on Okinawa. I lean over the rail, scanning the serene island, wondering about the bloody campaigns fought here two decades earlier. I imagine the hand-to-hand combat.

Top announces that we can venture ashore for three hours, "But no drinking or fraternizing with the women."

Soon a rickety bus bumps us to a town called Naha. Next to me sits a raucous buck sergeant whose name tag reads "McGee." I'm a Pfc., so I take the window seat. Like the old MacIntosh, he swears with every sentence. McGee stands about six feet tall, and from his rambling, I learn he is from Oklahoma.

McGee vows to get drunk. I stare out the window thinking sober thoughts of what lies ahead.

Naha seems tidy. People squat instead of sit. Saws work backwards, a pull rather than a push. Men hold boards with their toes as well as their hands. Beer and cola cans are cut, opened, and flattened, then hammered, pressed, and pieced into creative murals. Nothing wasted.

Three hours pass quickly and time comes to board the bus. McGee shows up a slobbering, obnoxious, ugly American. His ranting rules the ride.

I think of my mom. She would say, "Go down to the tavern and get your father to come home."

"Which bar?"

"Try Vahsen's. If he's not there, look in Manley's, or The Village Inn."

My face would burn as I'd enter the smelly dive, scanning the lonely, laughing faces.

"Dad, Mom wants you to come home."

I glance at McGee and feel the old rage rising.

I nickname him The Worm.

Long Term Commitment

On Thanksgiving Day, Captain Richard Mayo approaches. "Marsh," he says, "I went through your files and noticed your scores."

"Yes sir?" I feel a twinge of fear.

"And you've had two years of college," he says.

"Yes sir." He doesn't know that I flunked out of Westchester Community College. In my final semester I had a 1.19 average.

"You know," he says, "I graduated from West Point."

"Yes sir, I know. I grew up on the other side of White Plains, not far from The Point. My coach took me there in high school for a fitness award." Captain Mayo is genuine, not breaking eye contact. "I got my picture taken there with a senior cadet," I add.

"Is that right?"

"I also played on an American Legion all-star baseball team. We played against your varsity. We lost twenty-one to four."

Mayo smiles, nods.

I like the captain, and I can tell he likes me. He has a stainless steel backbone. I remember seeing him, along with his wife, in the base chapel at Ft. Riley.

Then he surprises me. "Marsh, how would you like to get out of here and go to West Point?"

I pause. "Sir, my grades were bad."

"It doesn't matter. I could get you a Battlefield Commission."

All I think of is the long-term commitment. "So, I'd go four years to The Point, and then I'd have a four year commitment afterwards. I could end up right back here."

"Why yes," he says, "that could happen."

"Thank you, sir, but no thanks."

"Okay, it's your choice. If you change your mind, let me know."

Captain Mayo turns and walks away.

As I watch his back disappear into the crowd, suddenly have a sinking feeling. *Some ships come to port often. Others come only once and are gone forever. My ship just left.*

Guard Duty

Sergeant D'Armitt wakens me before my turn to watch. "Marsh," he whispers, "get up. There's something under the steps."

It sounds like an urgent SOS. "Quick, go see what it is," he says.

Careless GIs often trash the large bunkers. Graffiti lines the walls with slogans like *Charlie never sleeps, will you? Signed, Louie from Brooklyn, 173rd Airborne.*

I shine a flashlight at discarded C-Ration cans under the entry steps. "It's a black scorpion about five inches long."

"Well, kill it."

"I don't want to."

"Kill it," he says, "and that's an order."

I pull out my bayonet and engage the creature. I wince as he dies stinging the blade.

It's two nights later, and I hear a commotion in the bunker. Cutro and Vito share the watch. I hear Vito shout, "Shoot it, Bobby, shoot it!"

"Shoot what?" Cutro asks.

"It's a cobra," Vito says as it hisses in his face.

Morning comes, then night again. D'Armitt and I walk outside the perimeter. A dozer crunches a path through the thick jungle. Without warning, D'Armitt squats and fires a single round from his M-14.

"What are you shooting at?" I growl after hitting the dirt. I scan the trees for movement.

"Got him," he says. "Let's go."

"Got who?"

We come upon a seventeen-foot-long python with a head the size of a first baseman's mitt.

Guard duty: two hours on, two off.

I see a flare go off about seventy-five meters out. *Could be VC crawling through the barbed wire.* I radio back to Sergeant Sprague: "Request permission to shoot."

"Permission denied."

"Well, then send me a starlight scope."

"I don't want to," he answers. The scope is heavy and bulky, like a cast-iron watermelon.

Sprague finally lugs it to the bunker from his jeep. "There better be some enemy out there," he says.

I squint through the scope and say, "It's a wild boar tangled up in the double apron fence."

"You made me come out here for that?"

"Sorry, Sprague, but we are on guard duty, you know."

Ed and the Incident

Ed Foster sports red hair, freckles, and a come-easy smile. A few days before Christmas, 1966, he's barreling his five-ton dump to and from the Laterite pit outside Bearcat. He spreads his load as usual. But this time the raised truck bed catches a telephone wire. Odd, he thinks. He looks in time to see the wire hit a wall.

The wall, a marker of some sort, falls over onto some children. Ed sits speechless. Screaming Vietnamese arrive to lift the structure and remove the lifeless body of a small boy.

The confusion escalates as scores of locals jabber in high-pitched voices and wail in unison. Ed understands none of it. He's in shock. A helpless boy is dead.

A week passes. A star-spangled review board addresses the issue and finds Ed innocent. It was an accident, they say.

The image of the crushed boy grinds into Ed's psyche. It doesn't go away in spite of Ed's transfer to another unit. Nor does the haunting image vanish as he operates heavy equipment all day.

Each morning he awakens to the image of the unmoving child.

Old Enough to Vote

On Wednesday, December 28, 1966, I am assigned guard duty at the Laterite pit. The day before, some of our men received sniper fire.

Furlow, posed with his tank crew, smiles and says, "I got in a firefight yesterday," as if he'd scored two touchdowns at his high school game.

After a quiet morning, a mess truck brings lunch. The brown plastic tray has sections for each portion. But it's really all the same. I take a spot on a nearby log. *I'm not hungry.* I'm thinking about home, my birthday, and that nobody knows I'm twenty-one and finally able to vote.

Next to me squats a scrawny Vietnamese man, arms folded across his belly, bent over and shaking. The temperature is near one-hundred degrees, and this man is shivering. A younger Vietnamese nearby says, "Him sick. Fever, three days. No eat." He makes motions like a mosquito biting his arm. "Oh," I say, "Malaria."

I turn to the man and hold out my tray, "You eat?"

He looks at my eyes, wondering if I'm playing a bad joke. "Eat," I say.

He slowly reaches for the tray to see if I'll pull it back. When he realizes I'm not kidding, he snatches it and devours the food without pausing for a breath.

I watch him take the bread roll and sop up the last bit of gravy. The entire meal vanishes in a matter of minutes. He shakes his head, a thank you.

When I turned seven, I received a green model car. I was so proud when I showed it to the family.

On my eleventh birthday, my mother bought me a trolley for my Lionel train.

When I turned thirteen, my dad surprised me with a silk bomber jacket.

But on my twenty-first birthday, I became a man, finally learning to give.

Feeling the Resistance

In a company of two hundred, you're bound to have at least one square peg squeezed into a round hole. Lionel MacKenzie III is that peg.

MacKenzie, a legend among our men, has an IQ of one hundred eighty. His baby-blue eyes always seem to be somewhere else in deep thought. MacKenzie takes his time responding, as if calculating even the simplest question. Like, "MacKenzie, where's your flack vest?"

"Huh?"

"Your flack vest."

"What about it?"

"Where is it?"

"My flack vest?" Then a long pause.

Sergeant Schook assigns him as a truck driver. To put a 5-ton dump in the hands of Lionel takes courage, but a better option than C-4 and blasting caps.

On Bearcat, the Ninth Division Communications unit arrives in late 1966 to set up telephone wires. Masses of pole climbers, like squirrels scurrying up trees. Men work day and night to string the compound in this crucial, critical event.

Meanwhile, the dump trucks rock around the clock in two twelve-hour shifts. The race is on to build roads, and Pfc. Matthison, a greasy biker, holds the record for loads of Laterite dumped in one day. He'll barrel in with a full load, raise the bed, and spread the dirt without missing a gear. The guy has finesse.

On his first day, MacKenzie gives it a try. Flying in, the bed lifts, the load spreads. Our cheering platoon in his rearview mirror urges him on. "Go, MacKenzie, go!" as he speeds toward the pit for another round.

One problem. He forgets to lower the bed.

Down the road he races, shifting until the dump bed catches some new wires. Snaps them off the poles. MacKenzie feels resistance. He downshifts for more power and traction.

A screaming pole-climbing posse pursues on foot, calling out oaths. Lionel catches the next wire, and then next.

The commo captain spits out his cigar and joins the chase, issuing curses that would curl the straightest hair. MacKenzie churns on, dragging wires, stretching them like guitar strings. The truck bed stands straight up, a salute to the parade behind.

The captain catches MacKenzie on the fifth wire when the truck slows to first gear. The captain curses and spits, and Lionel stands there taking it, eyes glazed, not even blinking.

I imagine MacKenzie transports himself to Michigan, reading the words of Socrates on his front porch as the captain rants.

Later he says, "Boy, that captain was mad."

"Yes, MacKenzie, he was mad."

Going Buggy

Someone on Bearcat gets the bright idea to hire local Vietnamese women to fill sandbags. Cheap labor. Only a jillion needed for the bunkers and squad tents. I've filled enough sandbags to dam up the Hudson River.

Since Top says we can't talk with the locals, we will need a liaison to supervise. Perhaps the lot will fall to Earl Waddell.

Waddell hails from Pawtucket, Rhode Island. We all wonder how he managed to get drafted at twenty-six and married. Most of us are twenty.

Waddell sits in the mess hall with his hand on his chin, and sighs. "I miss my wife." He pushes peas with his plastic fork. We worry about Waddell, losing weight, depressed.

Then Waddell notices a tiny black bug in the bread. Then another. I look at my slice. "I've got bugs too!"

Waddell announces to the entire mess hall, "There are bugs in the bread!"

Jimmie Wade of North Carolina says, "Them's weevils. Boll weevils. They didn't sift the flour."

Waddell begins a chant that everyone picks up. "There's bugs in the bread. There's bugs in the bread," we sing, fists banging on the table.

The chorus spreads until a hundred soldiers harmonize the bug song.

Waddell loses more weight over the next month. "I just can't eat," he says. "I miss my wife."

The CO figures Waddell isn't much good elsewhere, so the female sandbag detail falls to him. The crew turns out to be five young Vietnamese women who chatter like mice as they work.

The job proves low maintenance. Sit there and watch them. Waddell plays charades, learning to communicate.

Sometimes the girls take turns picking lice out of each other's hair. Nimble fingers work, separating stands. The lice are bitten and spit out with lightening speed.

Waddell says, "Aw, that's disgusting."

One day a girl catches a mouse. When she leaves for the day, she carries it by the tail, dangling.

Waddell says, "What are you going to do with that?"

She holds it over her mouth as if to say, "Eat it!"

Earl loses even more weight.

Dong Tam

Sunday, January 8, 1967. Captain Mayo stands in front of the company and announces, "Tomorrow we load up for Dong Tam. Have your duffle bags ready by 0600 hours."

"Dong Tam? Where is that?"

"The Delta. Our mission will be to prepare for the Ninth Infantry's arrival." His excitement spills over on us. It feels like a prison break after three months of hard labor and guard duty.

For the better part of the next morning we bounce along on B-24, one in a convoy made up of B and D Engineer Companies. "We're going to a party," MacIntosh says. "The only party is us. We're the advanced party."

We roll though the pristine town of My Tho. Women in silk dresses hold umbrellas leisurely in the marketplace. Where is the war?

We finally stop at the small beach, like a mini-Playland in Rye, New York. "Dig in," D'Armitt orders. "Set up your tents and make bunkers."

I look around at the skimpy sand pile. I note other companies, one Headquarters, one Signal, and one Infantry, all sharing.

Mayo says, "We'll build an air strip using PSP." Like running with razors in hand, we carry the pierced steel planks and build it at full speed. The strip looks like a large metal doormat, like several football fields joined together. It ripples when the C-130s land. We build a boat ramp to match. A civilian with a TV camera shoots our picture as we sprint. "Don't look at the camera when I film you," he says.

Kenny Fraiman says, "Let's all look at the camera when we go by."

I hear the man curse as he shut off the machine.

In the river floats the world's fourth largest dredge, the Jamaica Bay, a thirty-inch pipeline cutterhead dredge. Like a giant water vacuum, it spits up sand from the river floor to create land. The beach will become a city.

Locals are hired to fill sandbags and other menial tasks. The next morning I notice a Vietnamese man climb into the cab of a crane. *What's he doing?* He clutches a piece of paper, scribbling down notes. Eyes darting.

I say, "Captain Mayo, there's a VC spying on us." Mayo confronts him and takes him to his superior, Major George B. Anderson. "I saw him put the piece of paper in his mouth," I tell him.

Later I'm told swallowed whatever he was recording. The major says, "We interrogated him for hours. We did everything but torture him. We couldn't get him to talk."

On the night of Monday, January 9, into early the next morning, the dredge is hit by Viet Cong underwater demo men. Two American crew members drown. The "Sappers" slipped in, breathing through reeds, and set charges.

I know that guy had something to do with it.

"Engineer, Up!"

The Point Man comes upon a booby-trap. He issues a chilling cry, "Engineer, up!"

I squish my way through the mud to the front like a death row inmate walking "the last mile." After clearing everyone away, I kneel alone, stare at the Chinese grenade with the trip-wire tied to the pin.

In my head I can hear Schook's voice coaching me: "Crimp the blasting cap to the time fuse. Set the charge. Ignite the fuse, Yell fire in the hole. Walk away."

Some of us learn the hard way. Like Vito. One morning he is mine-sweeping a road ahead of some tanks. After a half hour the battery on his detector goes dead. He doesn't bother to stop and change it. Instead, he fakes it, going through sweeping motions.

The explosion behind him tells the tale. The lead tank hits a mine and track parts fly. The crew pours out like roaches when the lights come on. They're holding their ears and cursing Vito.

"I didn't think there were any mines on the road," he later says.

We tease him for a long time. "Tell us again, Vito, what Sergeant Schook said."

"Vito, you idiot. You stupid idiot."

The Playground

I finish fastening the final snap of our shelter in time to escape the sudden downpour. D'Armitt scrambles in, jockeying for elbow room. He fishes for his flashlight, bends over his notepad, and begins scribbling. I know it is his wife and kids that bother him.

"What are we doing tomorrow?" I ask as a small viper slithers between us, gone before I can scream.

"Why are you so jumpy?"

Jumpy? We just finished a day of mine clearing and short patrols.

"I don't like snakes," I say.

"They want us to build a playground tomorrow."

"A playground? That's funny."

We combat engineers are like the Army's foster children. Always attached but never belonging. Always on somebody's doorstep. Now we are with the Mechanized Infantry.

"We'll go on more patrols," D'Armitt says. "But for now, it's the playground."

At sunrise D'Armitt finds a spot under some large trees. Thirty of us clear the ground in no time. Up go the swings, fabricated with chains hanging from hooks on six-by-six stringers. Next a tire swing dangles from more chains.

"How will the kids know how to use them?" I ask.

"That's not our problem," D'Armitt says. "All we have to do is build it. You know, win the hearts and minds of the people."

That night the playground stands like an American child's dream: three swings, a slide from sheet metal, a jungle gym made from beams, and a tire swing to get dizzy on. The works. *Won't they be surprised.*

We fall asleep near the hamlet, lulled by the steady patter of rain hitting the tent.

The next morning I look forward to interacting with curious children. I step outside and look across the small field to the playground. It isn't there. Gone. Somebody must have slept on guard duty.

I say, "Hey, Sarge, it's not there."

"What's not there?"

"The playground."

Later, Captain Mayo and the other leaders assess the situation. "Local men probably came in at night and took the stuff," he says. "They had better use of chains and rubber and wood."

So much for surprises.

Breaking the Seal

In the Dark

I can't see my hand in front of my face. No moon. I bump into MacIntosh's backpack for the third time. The dust kicks up beneath my boots as we move in two files on a lonely road to who knows where.

Mac whispers, "I'll let you know if we stop."

To my right I hear the footsteps of the other platoon in file. *This is so crazy.*

I hear the panting around me. Suddenly one kid falls into a pit. His weapon, helmet, and entrenching tool make a clamor. "Help!" he screams.

I scurry across, grab his pack, and hoist him up.

"Quiet!" someone hisses, "you wanna get us killed?"

Another fifteen minutes pass, and I don't hear the men to my right. I bump into Mac again. He says, "Turn back. I think we took the wrong fork." Robert Bayly is in front of Mac. We start to retrace our steps double time, crashing into men following us.

The scene becomes bedlam. Men spin disoriented, pleading for help, begging not to be left alone in the darkness.

Mac says, "Follow me. Forget the noise."

We catch up to the men on the right and take the other fork.

Another thirty minutes pass. Up ahead, Sergeant Robinson is sitting in a jeep with the lights off. I hear his subdued command. "Line up along the road, face the field, and keep quiet. Spread the word." Then he adds, "Stand fifteen meters apart, and absolutely no talking. And don't move."

We pass the word and face the field, straining to see in the blackness.

Thirty minutes pass.

Waddell whispers, "Hey Marshy, you see anything?"

Mac is on my left. He says, "Shut up, we're not supposed to talk."

An hour passes.

At once, B-52 bombs drop along a tree line to our front. The sky brightens now and then. The impact of the concussion feels like a hard slap on my chest.

I hear someone to my left; he wants to stand near Mac.

"What are you doing?" Mac says. "You scared of the dark?"

"No," the voice says. "I just don't want to be alone."

A View from the Bridge

I'm sitting on top of a Bailey Bridge, a "Double-Double," overlooking a narrow, brown river. The lush green jungle foliage kisses the water's edge. No sign of movement. No dogs, birds, or fish. I'm already perspiring. I imagine February, back home in Port Chester. Mom's at work as a nurse. Dad's at Vahsen's Tavern having one too many. Silent snow is falling.

I balance myself astride the stiff girders, eyeing our stacked weapons below. Orders are to inspect the bridge for loose fittings. The sitting-duck aspect makes me nervous. I keep an eye, too, on the Vietnamese training camp 150 meters down the road.

Once again I look up. A soldier runs toward the bridge from the training camp. His green fatigues look like any other Vietnamese Friendly Force's garb. I see his white teeth, a smile or grimace, his black boots pounding like he's on the final leg of a 440-relay. Behind him, a close second, runs a similar looking soldier. I guess they're playing. A race, I tell myself.

Right below me, at the ramp, the trailing man tackles the front runner. You win. Game over. Shake hands and go away.

Without warning, the tackler kicks the man hard in the abdomen with his polished combat boot, knocking the wind out of him. The victim falls forward, clutching his belly. His body makes a puff of dust fly up around his skinny torso as he lands.

The pursuer kicks the fallen fellow's face. Blood spurts. A kick to the chest, to the face, to the stomach with black-belt swiftness.

I am sickened, frozen. I want to go home. Should I jump down and help? Help who? Who's the enemy?

The fight lasts thirty seconds but seems longer, like slow-motion. Blood and boots flying. I see disheveled black hair, head jerking, hyper-extending backwards. I think he's dead. I am separated from my weapon. I am separated from myself. I am insulated from the world.

A handful of Vietnamese soldiers appear. Each grabs an extremity. They lift him face up, spread-eagled. Yank his limbs. His bludgeoned head dangles and sways, like a hog toted to the roast. I watch as he's lugged towards the barracks.

I look back to our stacked weapons as the anger spreads through my body. These men should have been a rescue team, EMT's, angels of mercy. Instead, I am later told, the man was a Viet Cong, a traitor infiltrating the ranks, and swift justice was dealt.

My hands tremble as I go back to inspecting the bridge.

Who is the enemy?

Looking for Water

Dry Season, February 2, 1967. Operations with the 2nd/47th Mechanized. Three empty canteens bounce against my side as I walk around the tanks looking for a stream. Anything wet. Stagnant water would do. A puddle.

I envy the Mechanized Infantry. They have five-gallon cans of water strapped to each tank or Armored Personnel Carrier.

Word is: water will be dropped-in.

Sometime.

Today.

Tomorrow.

The day after.

No one knows.

I can't wait that long. My tongue feels like I've eaten peanut butter on Ritz crackers. Or like cotton candy in the Sahara.

I grew up on Long Island Sound with water everywhere. Rye Beach had two swimming pools. We had running water indoors. In the icebox, we had a tray with twelve ice cubes. Now, I dream of pressing my lips on the bathroom tap as I had done a thousand times growing up.

God, if I get to see a water fountain again, from now on I promise I'll stop and take a drink. I'll never pass another fountain.

Last night a kind-hearted fellow on a tank said, "I can't give you any water. We're not allowed to. But I have these hard candies you can take." *He's like an angel.*

"Thank you and God bless you," I said. "I'll never forget you." I sucked on them all night.

They saved my life.

But today, no angels. Men walk around like dazed vagrants. One guy says, "I'm going down this road to a farm house."

I say, "It's dangerous to go alone."

"I'm too thirsty, I don't care."

I notice to my left a tank with a bulldozer blade in back that's dug well into the dirt. I glance at the cannon, an Eight-Incher. I wander around the front. The angry sun reflects off the metal. No water there.

Without warning the cannon goes off. The thunderous explosion rattles every nerve in my body. I find myself flat on my face in the dirt, ears ringing, nerves screaming as if I've been struck by lightening. The tank rears up, stopped by the blade. The cannon lowers on pneumatic pistons, hissing their mockery as if to say, "How dare you walk in front of me."

I shake for an hour, still looking for water.

Finding Water

Sergeant D'Armitt announces, "We're still out of water." Yellow-brown sand blows everywhere. Men walk around with tongues hanging out, like dog day summers.

"Out of water," I say, fingering my canteens. "What will we do?" The thick, swirling dust churned by the Armored Personel Carriers mixes with sweat, forming a ready-made mud pack.

On foot, we pass a stagnant pool of green water. Some of the men say, "Let's fill our canteens."

D'Armitt shouts, "Don't touch that water!" I stand by, debating in my mind. *I'm so thirsty.*

Later that day, my buddy Gary Bayles from Ohio says, "I know how to get water." Gary is straight as a fence post, a solid, no-nonsense farmer. He tries to teach me about disking, planting, and harvesting. I have a hard time imagining what he's talking about.

"Bayles," I say, "explain how you can get water."

"I'm staying back from patrol. I'll dig for it."

"Dig? How deep?"

"Till I hit it."

I leave for a one day patrol with our engineer platoon. We fill canteens in the swamp; brown water poured through a piece of cloth to filter out sticks and sand. Add a few purification pills.

When I return that evening, Bayles is standing in a hole eight feet deep. Brown water up to his ankles. Men stand in line, waiting as he passes up the canteens.

"I told you I'd find water," Gary says.

Carry My Spool

We've walked only an hour. It smells of death. Something died out here. I shift the commo wire spool from my right hand to my left. The handle is slippery from my perspiration. My fingers feel numb, like they don't belong to me. The heavy mud reminds me of working out with ankle weights. My gait mimics one with Parkinson's.

Larry Furlow, five meters in front of me, shifts his spool. His has no handle.

"Marshy," he says, "how about trading spools."

Furlow is street-wise, born and bred in Newark's inner city. Six-feet two and boisterous. Big smile, big talker, the king of con men.

He recently told my friend Bayles, "If I ever see you out there alone, I'll shoot you."

If you were a Christian, you'd carry his spool.

"No," I say. "I'm not trading."

Throughout the patrol he keeps at it, "C'mon, Marshy, trade."

Should I carry it?

"No, I'm not switching."

Today the mosquitoes are like vampire bats in search of Type O blood. I've donned permanent blinders, like the horses near Central Park. I'm in survival mode.

Put in my year and go home.

I close up. I am at war within.

The things I don't want to do, I end up doing.

Who will set me free?

Becoming Hard

During our month-long operations with the 2nd/47th Mechanized Infantry, we're riding on armored personnel carriers. I like the idea of not walking. Like cruising Main Street in a classic car.

Up ahead, something in the road holds up the convoy. The tank commander shouts to the driver, "Get off the road and go through that rice paddy!"

I glance to my right and see two Vietnamese, a father and son, hard at work in the field. Each holds a handle on a rope with a large bucket between them. In rhythmic flow they scoop water from one field and sling it over the dyke to the adjacent paddy. Back and forth they move, never missing a beat, muscles glistening.

The driver hesitates. The tracks would destroy the dyke, and he knows it.

The commander shouts, "I said, get off the road and go around! This is war!"

The driver obeys the order. We plow ahead. I don't want to look.

But I do.

The water gushes into the lower paddy like a torrent. My cheeks burn. I look away.

The father and son stare; they scramble to close the breach.

A month later, I'm walking behind Donald Atwood. He's not a wise-guy like Furlow. Atwood carries a deflated rowboat with oars. When folded up, it forms a gigantic backpack, bulky and cumbersome. He looks like a sci-fi robot wobbling through the thick tropic swamp.

The raft begins to come undone. And I am coming undone. Atwood's brawny arms glimmer with sweat in the sunlight. He leans with all his weight, dragging it step by step.

Atwood asks, "Hey, Marshy, can you carry this for a while?"

If you were a Christian, you'd carry it.

I shake my head, "No."

My heart hardens, dry and crusty, like a lump of Play Dough left out overnight.

Atwood doesn't complain. He is shirtless, beaten. And I am doing nothing.

I am hard.

Monkey on My Back

Pfc. Friend and Spec.4 Silkey buy a pet monkey from a local scalper.

The daft, obese medic has one too. One night he rolls over in his sleep on his monkey and smothers it.

I ask, "Didn't you feel the animal squirming and struggling for breath?"

"No, I didn't," he says, giggling.

I want to ask, "What did you do with the body?" but I drop the subject.

Pfc. Friend named the monkey Fred after Silkey. Fred is playful; seems to live for antics. He won't bite you. The kind you never tire of watching. And he is curious. Too curious.

One night Fred snoops around the company mascot, a small German Shepherd.

At dawn, Friend grabs me. "Sergeant Marsh, you've got to come help me. Something's wrong with my monkey."

In the first light we stand staring at the wounded creature. He is listless, leaning to his right. His skull has teeth marks and he has fine tremors.

Friend's voice breaks. "We've got to do something," he says.

I say, "There's no hope for your monkey. We need to put him out of his misery."

"Should we shoot him?"

"Not here on the base camp. We'd have everybody running."

When I was seven I had a cat named Tippy. He ate rat poison in our basement apartment. He howled and flopped. My mother said, "Go get a shovel."

She walloped Tippy's head. Over and over she hit my cat. Wham! Wham! As I watched in silence.

"Friend," I say, "go get a shovel." Nearby, a fire simmers in a 55-gallon drum. The plan is to strike the creature and lower the body into the fire.

He says, "You do it."

I say, "It's your monkey," holding out the tool.

"You do it," he says. "Please."

I hold the long-handled shovel and raise it above my head. *Lord, make it quick.*

When I strike the suffering monkey's head, the shovel turns in my sweaty hands. It grazes him.

"Hit him again," Friend cries, "hit him again!"

I feel sick. One more, quick swat and it is over. We place Fred into the low, crackling flames.

Friend and I stand for a long time in silence, staring at the red and yellow embers.

Taking Charge of the Charge

Larry Furlow and I lie face down in the ditch. "Let me blow it up," he says.

"No. I'm in charge. I found it. I'll blow it up."

I glance back at the convoy. We've already held it up for fifteen minutes. They can continue to wait. With bayonets we probe, palms up, knives held as if they are living things, extensions of our fingers. Clearing away the dirt, I say, "It looks like about fifteen inches in diameter."

I look closer. "It's an anti-tank mine. Let's blow it in place. No sense disarming it."

The mines are shaped like birthday cakes, with three separate ways to detonate. The top center fuse is for a tank to run over. BOOM.

The side has a fuse like a trap. If the mine is twisted, BAM.

The third is hidden underneath, difficult to reach. If the mine is lifted, a small door like a mousetrap will spring, setting off the charge.

We are trained for safety first. Furlow sets the charge electrically instead of using a time fuse. Quicker.

With the wire in place, Larry yells, "Everybody clear away!" We take cover in the ditch. Furlow calls three times, "Fire in the hole!" Then he asks once more, "Marshy, can I blow it?"

"I want to do it," I answer.

I twist the handheld detonator. KABOOM!

A silver object tumbles through the air and comes to a landing, wobbling like a plate in front of us. We take an inspection. Our mine is nothing but a 1960 Chrysler Imperial hubcap, slightly bent, shimmering in the sun.

I lower my head.

I should have let Furlow blow it.

Rest and Recuperation

For most soldiers in Vietnam, the promise of R&R dangles like a carrot. Kind of like a furlough from prison for good behavior. The married men all want to meet their wives in Hawaii.

I request Taiwan because my brother-in-law, Peter, has an older brother named Anthony who lives in Taiwan. Anthony and his wife adopted twin Chinese girls.

But as with most military plans, I get assigned five days in Hong Kong instead. Before we make our way to the hotel rooms, beautiful prostitutes pair up with the GIs. One buxom beauty throws her arms around me and says, "Oh, handsome boy, you for free."

I slip out of her arms and walk briskly to the port.

I venture through Kowloon and find a place to eat. A bargirl sits by me. I ask, "Why do you sell your body?"

She looks at me with hollow eyes. "Why not?"

I steal away alone at the harbor, leaning for a long time on the rail. I stare at the docked white Russian ship. I flash back to the Russian box of supplies for the Viet Cong we found in the jungle. *Are the supplies going to Vietnam through China? Do the unloaded crates contain SKS rifles?*

Williams and Reynolds

Roger Williams from Kansas City perches atop his front-end loader and heads out from Bearcat on March 3, 1967. Specialist 5 Reynolds joins him. Since our engineers cleared the road, it will be safe indeed.

They each like to laugh. Williams has a fan club, including the cut-up Jimmie D. Inman. "That Williams is so cool," Inman says, "he dents his beer can so he knows where the hole is in the dark."

Everybody likes Williams. He reminds me of a country singer: slow talking, calm, witty. He smiles a lot, a southern drawl.

They barrel out the gate and bounce along the highway to the pit. They're traveling a bit too fast, but who cares? No police in these parts.

Without warning the loader jackknifes to the left, sending Reynolds flying to the right. He ends up in a ditch, shaken, but no broken bones.

The loader rolls over and crushes Williams. He's dead.

I get back from R&R that day and the first person I see is Reynolds. He is pale, lifeless. His voice cracks as he tells me the details.

"I just want to go home," he says.

Never Volunteer

I step on the bumper of the five-ton dump truck with the painted white ID marked B-24 and hop over the tailgate. Seven of us scramble, squeezing onto the open bed, jostling to get comfortable. The convoy cranks it up, clattering, spewing diesel fumes past our faces.

"I can't wait to get a hot meal," I say. "These Cs are killing me."

"I just want a shower and a cot," Bayly says, leaning over the cab.

As I stretch out on a pile of equipment, I hear the lieutenant say, "I need one man."

I think of my boss back in New York, Harold Valentine, a six-foot-three WWII vet. Before I got drafted, he called me into his office, giving me his quiet fatherly advice.

"Keep your mouth shut. Do what you're told. And never volunteer."

I ease my helmet over my face and feign sleep.

Never volunteer.

The lieutenant speaks louder. "I need one man."

No one moves.

"If none of you volunteer, I'm going to pick one."

Silence like a New England snowfall at midnight.

"Ok," he says, "Marsh!"

"Yes sir."

"Get off the truck."

"Yes sir."

"You're staying out another night."

I grab my gear and hop down, ignoring the snickers as I sling my weapon. "What am I supposed to do?"

"Go over to that tank and spend the night. Ride back with them in the morning."

"Yes sir."

"Hey, Marshy. We'll think of you tonight when we get a hot meal."

The tank rests in an open field, as obvious as an ink spot on white linen. I knock on the fender, feeling like a Fuller Brush man on a cold call. A head pops out of the turret.

"My lieutenant told me to spend the night on your tank. I'm supposed to ride back with you in the morning."

"Climb aboard," the voice says, "and make yourself at home."

I try to get comfortable on the steel fender. My soul sinks with the setting sun. What wrong have I done? I look up at the constellations and complain, "Why can't I go back?"

The squelch radio blares on and off for the next hour. One message gets my attention.

"We've got a hold-up in the convoy," the crackly voice says. "Claymore Mine. Vehicle B-24. Two casualties."

I bolt upright. "Hey, that's the truck I was on," I say to the men below.

"Really? B-24?"

"Yeah."

Suddenly the Milky Way seems closer. A sense of peace oozes over me, and for one night amber light from a million galaxies bathes my dirt-caked soul.

Roadside

The dust swirls like a dragon's tail, lashing my face as our convoy barrels through one hamlet after another. Pajama-clad Vietnamese line the roadsides mouthing bits and pieces of nonsensical speech. "GI, boom-boom, GI, chocolate..." Naked-bottomed children, hands outstretched, beg for treats tossed in their direction. Our 5-ton dumps rumble like runaway box-cars on a freight train. Pockets of men in black pajamas loiter in small groups. Allies by day, VC by night.

I notice a child bolt in front of us to retrieve a stray C-Ration can. Our driver doesn't see him. My boots smash the floor where I ride shotgun, like a Driver's Ed teacher hitting the brakes. "Look out!" I shout. The kid scuttles away untouched, but my nerves are frazzled.

This past week's Claymore incident with Quinn and Al Mack wounded on B-24 doesn't help either.

I cradle my rifle across my arm on the doorsill. Locked and loaded.

Ahead I see a young man, perhaps eleven or twelve. He winds up like Whitey Ford and starts to pitch a dark, round object in our direction. Again, my feet hit the floorboards and in one motion I arch from my seat, take aim, and flip the safety off. As quickly as he appeared, the boy pulls back his arm and doubles up laughing, holding up an olive drab meal can. In a second, he fades, vanishing in the sideview mirror. I ease back in the seat, feeling weak and clammy.

God help me, I could have shot a boy.

Who Will Lead the Squad?

My squad leader, Sergeant D'Armitt receives a letter that sends him reeling. His hands shake as he reads and re-reads his wife's cry for help.

"My daughter is running away from home," he says. "My wife's having a hard time."

"I'm sorry," I say and touch his shoulder.

D'Armitt has five children. "I've got to get out of here," he says. "I'm going to Top." He would plead his case like Perry Mason.

He returns with his head down.

"What did he say?"

"No go."

With Dong Tam and the Mechanized Infantry behind us, we have patrols with the Infantry next.

The following day, as D'Armitt talks with Top in the company area, he begins pacing in small circles around him. He's unraveling like a ball of twine. What do you do when a man cannot function? When he can't perform the simplest tasks?

Top has to release him. The following day, D'Armitt disappears with re-assignment orders in hand, escaping on the Freedom Bird.

How could you not pity him? He leaves a gaping hole in our hearts.

Sergeant Jackson asks, "Who wants to take D'Armitt's place?"

I shrug. "Spec. 5 Reynolds should be the squad leader," I say. "He's been in for thirteen years."

Reynolds, still shaken over Williams' death says, "My time is short. I don't want it."

I say, "Wallace, you take it. You've been in thirteen years, too."

"I can't take it," he says. "I've been busted down too many times."

I've been a Spec. 4 for a month. The following week, I am given a waiver and thrown into the buck sergeant's world.

How do you tell people much older and smarter than you what to do?

I approach Wallace in private. "Wallace, you can make me or break me. I need your help."

The "Governor" scratches his chin, pauses, and smiles, "Little One, I'll help you."

He, too, watches my back.

Metamorphosis

As Providence would have it, McGee shows up in our squad three months after the bus incident. I still don't like him, but I notice that he says whatever is on his mind. You don't have to second guess.

Soon McGee receives a letter that sends him into a tailspin. He says, "My wife is having an affair with a friend of mine." Like our predecessor D'Armitt, he too begins pacing.

Top takes his weapon. "Go to bed."

I approach McGee lying on the cot and sit beside him. The tent sides are rolled up in a futile attempt to invite any faint breeze. McGee lies there, his nose flaring like a bull about to break through the fence.

I'm afraid to say anything, so I pray for words. None come. My own heart needs help. *Lord, forgive me for my resentment and anger towards him. What do I know? I'm single. What does war do to a married man with trouble at home? Look what it did to D'Armitt.*

My head is still down when McGee asks, "Are you praying?"

For myself, not for you.

I nod.

McGee turns away. I figure he's asleep, so I tiptoe out.

The next day something happens. McGee quits drinking and his language clears up. He becomes a model soldier. McGee isn't angry anymore.

Neither am I.

The worm turns butterfly.

Vito, You're Sick

Captain Mayo stands starched in front of the company and announces, "We're going out on patrols tomorrow. Some of you might not make it back." The smell of diesel fuel blends with the greasy aroma of the mess hall.

Vito paces. "If I don't make it back," he says to Cutro, "tell my mom and dad I love them." Vito is an electric guitar, strings wound tight and amps cranked up.

Mayo asks the Chaplain to minister to the needs of the men. Wetzel, a gentle, balding priest from St. Louis answers the call. "All those wanting to go to confession," he says, "line up here."

Vito is first. Men who never attend services line up behind him. Wetzel reminds me of those pictures of St. Francis of Assisi who had birds landing on his shoulders. Vito spends the evening scribbling last letters to Brooklyn.

In the morning, Mayo reads the plan. "Two engineers for each Infantry platoon." You could hear a pin drop. "B Company, 4th/47th. A Company, 3rd/39th."

Soon the Hueys whisk us away. Frankly, I'm ready.

After two months in the field, we fly back for a short respite. I stand talking with Vito and Cutro.

"Vito," Bobby asks, "What did you do out there?"

"Blew up a few things. Oh, and I shot a dead VC."

"You mean you killed one?" Bobby asks.

"No, he was already dead."

Cutro and I look at each other. Bobby tilts his head, like a pupil in the front row trying to understand a problem on the board.

"Vito, you shot a dead body?"

"Yeah." Vito lowers his head.

"Why did you shoot a dead person?" Bobby asks, moving closer to his face. Cutro isn't acting like Joe McCarthy, more like Carl Jung.

"I wanted to see how it would feel."

I look at Cutro and could see his pain.

Bobby squares off with him. "Well, how did it feel, Vito?"

"I felt sick. I mean, really sick."

"You are sick, Vito. Really sick."

"Yeah, I wish I never done it. I can't get it out of my mind."

Some Things Won't Work

I've been keeping my eye on Sergeant Reedy during the patrol. He stands three men ahead of me, leaning on a tree that seems scrawny next to his bellowing body. Like a beached whale, he flounders, pants, and gasps. "I just can't make it," he says to the squad, to the the world.

I plop my forty-pound mine detector kit in the mud and sit on it like I'm posing on a Samsonite at the airport. Reedy's soaked sleeping bag turns into an unraveling, waterlogged load. I see it coming, his strength waning, step by ragged step. Reedy and his torturous sleeping bag, undone.

This isn't working.

We've been here a while, like bumper-to-bumper rush hour heading out on the Brooklyn-Queens Expressway.

My mind drifts back to last week. We complained, "Our uniforms are moldy and our boots won't dry out." The enemy, mildew, crept in broad daylight, attacking everything, stealing what little creature comfort we had.

Captain Mayo said, "Turn in your stuff to Supply. Pick up your new jungle boots and fatigues."

It felt like Christmas without the wrappings.

That same week our trusty, accurate, too bulky, too heavy, and too prone to rust M-14s head for extinction. Enter the Mattel-looking M-16.

Reedy dabs his face and neck using a towel draped upon his shoulders like a green viper. He removes his helmet and wipes his forehead with a wet sleeve, then takes a swallow from his canteen.

When the new bladder canteens come out, I am the first taker. Invented to hold twice the capacity of a standard canteen, I say, "I'll take two."

One problem though. The first day I use them, the long thorns prick through the flimsy skin, causing my precious water to spray out. I say to the medic, "Quick, please hand me a Band-Aid."

"Here," he says, "but it's not going to work."

He is right. If Mac hadn't had compassion, I might have died.

Now Reedy straightens up and says, "We'll set up here for the night."

I think of the nouveau hammocks equipped with mosquito netting. How exciting to string them between trees.

At night the tide comes in, the trees bend, and the red ants are furious. I wake up in a jackknife position, feet straight up, buttocks soaking in the water.

It isn't long before Reedy is re-assigned to the States. For him, it didn't work.

One other thing doesn't work: the unconventional war itself. No fronts, no lines of delineation, hit and miss tactics. It could go on forever.

Some things will never work.

Sorting Out

"Does anyone want my bread?" I hold out the small, olive drab can. No takers. I stuff the next one, ham and limas, into my green tube sock.

When I first saw Reedy sink, he said, "I just can't make it." Sure, he was obese, but his pack didn't help.

Travel light.

Bayles and I work in silence.

The sorting out of the precious from the worthless becomes a vital daily chore when the choppers drop the goods and disappear.

Prioritize. Water comes first, three canteens full.

Next, ammo, M-79 with bandoliers, and .45 caliber pistol with clips.

Food follows. Push the Cs into green socks. Tie them to the front of the rucksacks. Let them dangle like long snouts on lumbering elephants.

After that, five pounds of C-4, time fuses, blasting caps, firing devices, and waterproof matches.

Don the jungle boots without socks. Always have the helmet, flak vest, and dog tags, not forgetting mosquito repellant.

No underwear, towel, or soap.

No bedroll. Sleep on a plastic poncho.

Prioritize.

Travel light.

Search and Cordon

Our convoy stops at a hamlet in the middle of nowhere. Typical village, grass huts side-by-side like a third world subdivision. Children everywhere, entertained by the giant-looking, round-eyed Americans.

A twinge of tension fills the air. Sergeant Roberts says, "Marsh, go in that hut and look for VC."

I feel like I am the batboy at Yankee Stadium being asked to pinch hit.

I hesitate at the bamboo door. Strange thoughts enter my head. *Should I knock? Or should I kick it in and shout, "This is the FBI! Freeze!"*

Roberts shouts, "Get in there!" I want to ask him why he doesn't want to go in. The flimsy door swings open at the touch of my hand. I step in. Seated around a low table are women ranging in age from eight to eighty. They sit still, hands in laps, heads lowered like Asian dolls.

With a round in the chamber and the safety off, I ask, "Men?"

They shake their heads, "No." It looks staged. I look around. The men of the hamlet saw us coming. They're probably hidden in underground tunnels, or they fled to the nearby jungle. I lift a lid of what looks like a tunnel, or a storage area. Strain to listen. No wonder the men ran. How would I feel if a foreign soldier came into my house when I was there with my parents?

I leave the way I came.

Sorry for disturbing your dinner.

Detaching from the Spool

D-Day

It feels like D-Day. Dark, 0330 hours, early March. The Mike boat slaps cool waves in the South China Sea, and a fine salt mist like snake spit sprays my neck. To my right squirms Jimmy Burroughs, an intense, prissy fellow cracking his knuckles. On his right, GoGo Gross, his side-kick, who covers his face with his helmet. At my left, fellow engineer Kendrick drifting off to sleep.

To our rear fades our floating home, the USS Benewah, like a mother hen letting her brood find their own way. MacIntosh and Bayly are in the craft ahead of us. I imagine Mac jabbering. Thirty men on each Monitor Boat, ready for Normandy. Instead of beaches and cliffs, we will hit lush mangrove swamps. The ride takes almost three hours.

With sunrise, men stir in chilly whispers. I embrace my M-79 and adjust the bandoliers, making sure the safety is on, with a round in the chamber. I do the same for my .45 caliber Remington.

Lieutenant Heller says we'll move in three files.

Soon the vessel rams the banks and the iron grating lowers to form a ramp. I feel like Jonah leaving the whale at the shore of Ninevah.

I'll sprint a 40-yard dash and find cover.

I'm near the front, right behind a nice kid named Chili. Instead of a run, we walk two steps and sink just below the knees in the foulest, most malodorous muck imaginable. I have to lean forward to free my feet.

In the P.T. test at Ft. Jackson, I held the base record for the forty yard low crawl: fifteen seconds. No record today. It takes the platoon near half an hour to disembark. Already I'm exhausted.

The green foliage is missing, like trees stolen by clear cutters. Lieutenant says, "This place has been defoliated."

We walk all day and see nothing. No enemy. No sign of life.

This is not D-Day.

This is not Normandy.

Bird Dog

I hear a sound that brings me back to Armonk Airport when I was nine, clinging to the fence and looking up. Is it a Piper Cub? The sound doesn't fit out here. It's like hearing an ice cream truck jingling in the middle of the desert. I scan the sky and see a small, single-engine plane pulling up and almost stalling. Then it falls into a dive.

"What is he doing out here?" I ask.

"Don't you know? That's a Bird Dog, man."

"What is he doing?"

"It's a spotter plane. They spot the enemy and fire Phosphorous so the jets can bomb."

"Oh."

Later I learn the proper name is Forward Air Controller, or FAC.

The jets fly over five hundred miles an hour. The Hueys, over one hundred miles an hour. The FACs: well, they crawl just above the treetops. Sitting ducks.

How brave does the pilot have to be? These warriors are a rare breed. No heavy armaments. They seek out the enemy and direct the fire power.

Suddenly I feel a little safer.

I'm glad they're here.

Pistol Perils

"My pistol fell in," I say.

"We have to keep moving," Lieutenant Heller replies. We are on the trail of a squad of VC. No time to stop.

Some days we cross five or six rivers. Small ones, only as wide as my bedroom. Rapid flowing, dirty brown tidal water.

Atwood had inflated a rubber raft to transport our gear across. I piled on my rucksack with two others. One push and my Remington .45 slid from the holster. PLOP. Down it sank.

I dive down about eight feet and feel around the soft mud. For a moment I think of digging for clams under the float at Oakland Beach in Rye, New York.

I come up empty. Down again. Nothing.

Heller says, "You'll have to pay for the weapon."

"Why?" I ask. "This is a combat situation. Can't I say that it's a combat loss?"

I dive once more. Nothing.

Lieutenant Heller says, "It's not a combat situation. You have to be under fire to count it a loss. Just chasing the VC is not receiving fire. That's about five hundred-something dollars."

I don't have the money. I don't think it's right that I should have to pay. Just chalk it up as a combat loss.

"We didn't receive fire," he adds.

The machine gunner, Russ, looks like he could play middle linebacker for USC. He says, "I'll take a dive."

The lieutenant says, "Better hurry, we don't have much time."

Atwood keeps ferrying the remaining rucksacks. I will wait till the last man makes it over.

Russ comes up empty-handed.

"Thanks for trying," I say. "Just forget it."

"Let me try one more time," he says.

I can't get over the thought that with all the waste in this frustrating war, I would have my feet held to the fire over a measly pistol.

The lieutenant persists. "If they were pursuing us, you could count it as a combat loss."

Suddenly, Russ splashes to the surface. Pistol held high. He gasps and smiles.

"Thanks," I say. "You saved me five hundred dollars."

"Move out," the lieutenant says.

Illusions

At sunrise on the third day of a patrol, Lieutenant Heller says, "We're going back by Mike boats."

The point man, Larry Aden, says, "I see the masts of a ship." To me it is like a rainbow pointing to a pot of gold.

Heller says, "The map shows our pick-up area is straight ahead." We all step up the pace.

"Looks like a few thousand meters ahead," Atwood says.

Piece of cake. We move out in a hurry.

By ten o'clock we take our first break. "How far is it now?" GoGo Gros asks.

Lieutenant looks at his map, then to the masts, and says, "Shouldn't be too far now."

Atwood says, "Another thousand meters." The masts peek just above the trees on the horizon. The sun seems higher already.

Why aren't the ships getting closer?

In high school I earned letters in football and baseball. In a fitness test involving over one hundred high schools in the New York City Metro Area, I placed eighth. It means nothing now. Out here, the playing field is level. We are all dead tired.

The mud becomes deeper, heavier on my boots. Jimmy Burroughs says, "Look, there's a dead alligator in that ditch." Or did he say tiger? I'm too tired to think. Gros moves to look. I pass.

By noon, Heller spreads the word, "Break for lunch."

I flop into the mud. *My athletic training means nothing.* While digging into meatballs and beans, I talk with Krietlow, a former gymnast. Sitting in the mud, he takes me through the steps of how to do the *Valdez*, a tricky floor exercise move.

Where does he get his energy? What's wrong with me?

In twenty minutes we move out again. The ship masts look closer, for sure. "We're almost there," Atwood says. Some men break into a run.

At 2 p.m. I'm about to fall out. I can't keep up. *I can't take another step.*

Just then, the lieutenant shouts, "Take ten!"

I collapse in the mud. We're still not there. Are we seeing a mirage? Maybe the masts aren't really there. Maybe we're seeing things.

Some of us athletes, some office boys.
All following an optical illusion.
All are the same.
All are dead.

Friendly Fire

We're hacking our way through dense jungle. Without warning, bullets begin flying overhead, cracking like lightning bolts and tearing off branches. In seconds, we're clawing dirt.

"Those sound like fifty caliber machineguns," the lieutenant shouts. Limbs fall around us like an October lumberjack festival. "They must be coming from the Monitor Boats," he says.

"Hey," I say, "Somebody's gonna get hurt."

I want to grab a mic and broadcast to the world: *Bullets hurt! Tree limbs, human limbs, all alike.*

We usually pull each other out of the muddy stream beds by using the muzzles of the M-16s after asking, "Is the safety on?" One man in another platoon shot and killed his buddy trying to help him out of the water. The understatement was, "Yeah, they said he was real torn up about it."

Another day our 15th Engineer patrol tromps through heavy undergrowth. An F-105 nicknamed Thud zooms upon us just above the treetops. So fast they can't be heard approaching. Each wing fires 20mm cannon rounds that sound like an old man with a bad case of the croup. Everyone dives for cover when the pilot mistakes us for Viet Cong. *Can't he see we're Americans?*

The afterburner's roar deafens.

He makes another pass. I hear the coughing again, then the screams. Fear and panic. My fingers claw into mud, and my neck strains to keep my steel pot still.

To my left, a squad hacks its way toward us. One rosy-cheeked kid with his helmet tilted sideways pants, "Look at my M-16 stock. It's shattered."

Two others say, "Look at our canteens." I finger the holes in each. Another has a piece of shrapnel lodged in his pocket New Testament.

I look up and see the pilot do a Victory Roll.

Friendly fire.

The Japanese Are Coming

Three small, muscular Japanese TV reporters move with an air of confidence as they leap from the choppers. They chat in low tones as they fumble with a telescopic tripod and a grotesque movie camera weighing at least sixty pounds. The camera has two large covered Mickey Mouse-looking ears on top. I take them to be concealed 35mm reels. One shrouds the contraption in clear plastic.

Three days out here, fellows, and the mildew will eat that thing alive.

After a few minutes, I realize they can't speak English. I certainly don't know what "Anatawa icu" means, but I know how to play charades. They nod. They bow. They begin the walk.

During the first hour it becomes obvious that nothing matters but one small issue. Not the enemy. Not the heat. Not thirst or mosquitoes. Certainly not the film shoot. It is all about the mud.

The man in front of me strains to lift his right leg, like a mini-Sumo wrestler stepping toward his opponent. His face grimaces. He says something in Japanese that sounds like "Dang!"

After the second hour the scene turns sour. Scrap the six o'clock show.

The little man gives his best, but the swamp has him against the ropes. He sinks to his shins, calling for help. His two friends in front can only turn and look. They share the same plight. The cameras have to go.

The lieutenant radios for a dust-off, an act of mercy. Tokyo would have to wait for a more palpable scene. Three Japanese filmmakers leave as they came, all jabbering in unison as they move to a clearing, ready to board the chopper.

How do you say "mud" in Japanese?

Someone's Watching Us

The peeking sun lights the sleepy jungle foliage with soft shades of pastel green. I roll onto my hands and knees and blink, stretching like a lazy cat. Botanical garden dream. I've developed a love-hate relationship with the mangroves. I'm captivated by the aesthetics, yet despise the red ants, mosquitoes, and snakes. The elusive Viet Cong are a nagging nuisance, a bad tooth.

In this war, silence is king, and hyper-vigilance reigns. I compress my plastic poncho into a compact jellyroll and secure it to my rucksack, keeping one eye out for anything suspicious.

The platoon stirs, speaking in whispers. "How many Klicks are we going?" The other day we walked only one Klick in ten hours.

James Fox comes close and says, "I'm traveling light. I'm getting rid of my poncho." He tosses it in some thorny bushes.

Point man, Larry Aden says, "I'm throwing away my machete sheath. It keeps banging against my leg." He pitches it aside.

I look at my 35mm Minolta. Why did I bring it out here? I'm going to junk it. Instead, I peel off the leather cover with my name scribbled inside and fling it on the litter pile.

We move out by sun up, walking in columns. "Five meters apart, one round will get all of you." In a low stream a viper wiggles through my legs. I scream and jump. Lieutenant Heller says, "What's the matter? I thought you guys from New York were tough."

"We don't have snakes in Port Chester," I answer.

No snipers or booby-traps after a day's march in ankle deep mud and forking brown rivers. Strange. Too quiet. We arrive at a point on the map where two rivers meet, like coming to an intersection on an avenue. I imagine myself in New York, hiding on a rooftop or ducking in an alley. If unwary Viet Cong came walking down the street, then I'd have the upper hand.

We arrive at the ambush site at dusk. Twenty or so Chinese hand grenades stand on bamboo sticks, spread out in a circle, like candles on a cake. Each shoot is pressed into the soft mud, camouflaged. Fishing wire is attached to the pins. The wires are stretched taut, secured to trees like a cat in the cradle.

A green engineer with me starts to help. "Marsh, I'll pull them up for you." He begins yanking on a stick.

I lose it and start screaming, "No! Don't touch anything!"

Too late. Others have pulled some up.

I clear everyone away and cut the wires near the pins. After all are cut, I sit with my back against a tree and look at the scene. My heart stops. In the middle of the circle of booby-traps rests a neatly stacked pile of wares: Fox's poncho, Aden's machete sheath, and my camera cover.

"Lieutenant Heller, they're watching us."

"What do you mean?"

"Look here. We threw this stuff away this morning. We're being followed."

By now it's too dark to blow them up. We carefully make a pile of twenty grenades on sticks. I lay down next to them, bizarre bedfellows.

The Viet Cong are watching us.

The Conscientious Objector

I'm sitting in the latrine on the USS Benewah after lights out. There's just enough light to catch up on my small stack of mail. I hold a letter containing an obituary. "A friend of mine got killed in a car wreck," I say. "Stephen Dolan. I grew up with him. Here we are in a war zone and my classmate dies at home."

A Pfc. named Richard, sitting next to me on a commode, says, "I just got this letter about a friend of mine too." He holds it up. "He was killed here in Vietnam. Somewhere up north. I hate it."

"Dolan was a nice kid," I say. "What a shame."

"Yeah," Richard says, "My friend, too. We grew up together." Richard's cheeks flush. "I don't like this war," he says, lowering his brow and staring at the handwritten note.

"So who does?"

"I mean, I don't like it at all." His tone is stern.

"I just want to get home," I say.

"I think I'm a conscientious objector," Richard says.

"What? You are not. You were out in the field."

I couldn't help thinking back to January 11, 1966, at Whitehall Street in Manhattan. I stood in line at the Induction Center. In front of me was a tall, long-haired guy wearing bell bottoms. "I am a conscientious objector," he said.

The sergeant at the desk said, "Oh, yeah?" They whisked him away to another room and the hair on the back of my neck stood up as I heard shouting and loud thuds.

Richard folds his letters and repeats his newly declared philosophy. "I believe I am a conscientious objector."

"You are not," I say. "You carried a rifle."

I recall my two-week Leadership School at Ft. Leonard Wood. A nice fellow from California, Pfc. Lomeli, slept across from me. One night he said, "I don't want to kill another human being." He talked about it day and night. Pfc. Williams and I tried to reason with him. Lomeli argued. Lost sleep. During the second week, his mind broke and he ended up in the Psychiatric Ward at the base hospital.

The morning after our bathroom conversation isn't pretty.

Richard tells Heller, "I am a conscientious objector. I refuse to kill my fellow man."

This causes no small stir among the men of B Company, from the brass down. The hair again stands up on the back of my neck when they yell at him.

Richard is made to walk point for three days without a weapon. For that I give him credit.

Then he was gone.

Conscientious.

Objector.

Report Back to Me

E7 Sergeant Jackson, our tall Lifer platoon leader, gives me the same orders each week: "Here's five pounds of C-4. When you get back to the ship, report what you use." Jackson rests his elbows on the bunk and smiles.

I say, "Sure, Sergeant. See you in three days."

After a month of three day patrols, I ask, "Sergeant, are you ever going out, too?" His smooth face glistens, his hair slicked back like he's ready for a wedding. I smell fresh cocoa butter.

"Are you kidding?" he says. "I'm not going out there. I'm married. I got kids." Then he laughs and looks at me sideways.

"Oh." *Guess I missed something.*

Top Sergeant doesn't care either. Nobody cares.

I find myself wishing to stay with B Company, 4th/47th. Lieutenant Heller bonds with his men. Sergeant Johnnie Jones is always right there and proves himself as a leader. They care about each other.

Meanwhile, the USS Benewah yaws under our feet from March till May. It becomes a cozy home, moored off the Vung Tau harbor.

Week after week, Jackson hangs around his bunk, looking into his small round mirror. He uses tweezers to pick out stray hairs from his chin. Each day, Jackson browses the ship's store, plays cards, or reads. He hangs out with his platoon sergeant buddies and listens to music.

It never bothers me to hand out some small balls of C-4 for cooking. Shireman, "The General," always has his hand out first. I don't care if we don't find booby-traps to blow, so what? Who cares? If I need some to blow one in place, the men will donate theirs back.

I'll tell Jackson, "I blew a few booby-traps today. I don't have any C-4 left."

After patrol we stand on the pontoons while a sailor blasts away the mud with a fire hose. Once aboard, I strip and head for the shower. On the way I hear some guys talking. "That Jackson is a coward. What do you think, Marsh?"

"I don't care."

Perception Is Everything

Ten choppers hover over the landing zone after circling. I sit at the open door, feet dangling in the wind. Three F-100s dive like birds swarming a cat.

The door gunner shouts, "Get ready to jump!"

"Aren't they gonna stop bombing?" I ask. The Huey rotors hum their familiar song, the blades slapping time.

Our helicopter is the last in a row of ten. Smoke fills the LZ. Behind me sits Kendrick, yawning as if he is riding to the grocery store in the family sedan.

"Gee," I say, "I hope we don't get near the Napalm." I can see trees burning below as jets pass.

"Nah," Kendrick says.

The door gunner aims his M-60 and fires away. "Go!" he shouts. I figure about an eight foot jump. "Can't the pilot get any lower?" I ask.

"Go!' he screams.

Out I go. The weight of my gear adds speed to my descent. Behind me Krietlow twists his ankle and shouts, "I can't walk! Call a chopper back!"

Lieutenant Heller says, "Aw, you're just trying to get out of the patrol."

I scramble for cover, moving from tree to tree, frantic for somewhere to hide. I can see the writing on the missiles. I turn to check on Kendrick and can't believe my eyes. He is sitting on his helmet, opening a can of C-Rations. Napalm burns behind him.

I yell, "Kendrick, take cover!"

One black bomb springs its fins and floats down, wobbling. I can see the lettering on it. It passes to my right, landing in the middle of the platoon. I brace myself for the explosion. Debris flies straight up as if an invisible force forms a cylindrical wall around the shrapnel.

Heller gets on the box screaming, "Cease fire!" and some other choice words. A miracle no one is hurt. I think we are in Dante's Inferno.

"What are you so afraid of?" Kendrick asks, scooping another mouthful.

"What am I afraid of? What do you think those jets are dropping?"

"Aw," he says.

I squat under a tree and stare at Kendrick. He is digging his plastic spoon in his ham and limas as if he's attending a family picnic in Hartford. Lately I notice that he's started talking to himself. Not out loud, but I can see his lips moving like a ventriloquist without a wooden dummy. He seems self-contained, self-absorbed.

Should I be afraid? Or does my imagination magnify my fears? Is Kendrick right?

Three days later we head back by helicopters. It looks like we're rising higher than usual. I lean over to look at the altimeter. Nine thousand feet. "Why are we going so high?" I ask.

"We're receiving ground fire," the pilot says.

I notice they are sitting on flack vests. I lean forward again and shout to the pilot, "Can we go any higher?"

Behind me Kendrick says, "Aw. What are you so scared of?"

Perception is everything.

Wasted Money, Wasted Effort

Something's wrong with the bilge pump," Lieutenant says. Chili and I cling like spiders to the front grail on the Mike Boat. The spray from the South China Sea is exhilarating as the vessel bounds over green waves.

I turn to look at the twenty-eight men sitting in eight inches of water. Heads are down, staring at the sloshing mess. Our new engineer lieutenant says, "Happy Easter."

"You're kidding," I say. "What's the date?"

"Sunday, March 26th."

My family will be in church. Well, maybe not Dad. Americans all dressed up.

As we approach the USS Benewah, Heller says, "Everyone throw your ammo over the side."

"What for?" Tucker says.

"Just do it."

GoGo whispers, "One round of an M-16 costs fourteen cents." Over the side they go. Hundreds of rounds, jettisoned. Good thing I carry the M-79. I'll keep my grenades. Maybe the brass is no good after days in the swamps.

A week later, Befort's squad finds a small cache of weapons. One piece is an old French recoilless rifle left over from the French-Indo China War.

Heller radios back and reports the find. Word comes to ditch the small arms and carry the recoilless back as proof. I think Heller will at least make front page in the *Old Reliable* newspaper.

Machine gunners Russ and Hoy, the chosen two, will tote the monstrosity. These men are strong and able but a comedy of errors, indeed. They tie a bamboo stalk to the long rifle and carry it like a dead carcass.

Trouble is, the Rung Sat is hostile. They slip and slide for a day and a half, carrying it across rivers and through the hateful mud.

The prize rides back on the Mike Boat. When we moor alongside the USS Benewah, a major dressed in pressed fatigues and shiny boots stands on the pontoon. *He looks just like the guy who interrogated the VC in Dong Tam.*

He says, "Yep, that's an old French recoilless rifle all right. You can throw it over the side." He retreats up the gangplank and stands on the deck.

I tune the man out while I am hosed down. Bill Wolters quotes the major as shouting from the deck, "Move like you've got a purpose!"

Three days in the swamp. Was that, too, a wasted effort?

Mean Streak

We stand by a river at midday, breaking for Cs and a smoke. A Hawaiian staff sergeant talks with other squad leaders of his platoon. I am assigned to them for three days.

I nickname him Lizard. He squints with a sinister smile, fiendish, like a crocodile baring his teeth.

Hundreds of crabs dot the muddy banks, scrambling sideways here and there. I've gotten used to them crawling under my poncho at night. With an arch of the back I think, *C'mon, little fellows, scramble by.*

I watch Lizard take a cigarette and place it in a large crab's claw. "Look," he says, "he's smoking. Ha-ha."

I must endure this for another day.

Men laugh. I stare at his Sardonic sneer. He's pleased with his own sick humor. Unflinching, he yanks off the crab's legs one by one, tossing them in the river. Then he hurls the suffering crab into the water.

I want to say, "Hey, Sergeant Lizard Mean Streak, stop it."

Instead, I say nothing, biding my time until tomorrow and my next assignment.

The Thing in the Water

Larry Aden says, "Look here, these wires are sticking out."

We stand around the small muddy bunker facing the wide river.

"Looks like a VC command post," Heller says.

I tell Aden, "Don't pull on that bamboo thing. It could be booby-trapped."

My engineer lieutenant, the new guy, pulls them up and follows the wires into the water. "Somebody bring me an inflatable mattress," he says. "We're going out there." I like him, fresh out of Officer Candidate School, quiet, but confident. He says, "I'll swim and pull on the wire, you float on the raft and coil it up."

Sounds simple enough. At first, I straddle the rubber mattress like a surfer, trying to lie down the way I've seen them do on TV, paddling with one hand. But a rubber raft is not a board.

After a few minutes, the yards of wire get cumbersome. The enemy tied bricks to the wire as anchors. One by one they slip off the raft. I jump into the brink, trying to hold the mattress and retrieve the bricks, struggling to stay afloat. The lieutenant swims a few yards ahead of me, flinging the bricks my way.

With all my strength I pull myself up on the mattress with my belly draped in the middle, my legs dangling and kicking the water. By now we're fifty meters out. A swift-boat cruises nearby, curious about the oddball on the raft.

That's when it happens. I glance over the edge of the mattress and see a giant, coiled reptile THING with thick colored bands like rings down its body. It heads for my feet and I feel something solid brush against my boots.

"There's a THING in the water!" I yell.

I push the raft toward the lieutenant and break for shore, setting a record in the fifty meter freestyle.

I hear the lieutenant calling, "Where are you going?"

All I say is, "The THING!"

The Navy is right there picking up the lieutenant, bricks and all. Attached to the end is a large black ball with plug-like fuses around it. The lieutenant is the hero who found the mine.

Sometimes it takes only one event for a new man to prove himself. And I am out to prove nothing.

Step Where I Step

Thousands of men from the Commonwealth of Puerto Rico serve in Vietnam. They often argue about what part of the little island they live, like the Yankee-Rebel debate.

"I'm from San Juan," one says.

"Oh yeah, I'm from Mayagues."

"You're a cowboy."

I grow to like Jose Ramirez. He's a quiet guy with a coy smile, like he knows some grand secret that he'd tell only you. A decent fellow, polite. Whenever he gets scared or surprised, he'll blurt, "Abuela o tia!"

I ask, "What does that mean?"

"Grandmother or aunt!"

Jose tells me, "I grew up in the mountains near Rio Piedras. I used to walk in El Yunque." He describes the magnificent rain forest, with trees towering to the sky like a thousand church steeples. I call Jose "Jungle Expert."

Jose knows which plants are poisonous or edible. "You see this green stem?" he says. "You can cut it and drink fresh water from the bottom."

On patrols during the monsoons, the mud seems inaccessible, but Jose knows where to place his foot. Jose knows I need help. He paces like a gazelle, with an uncanny way of avoiding booby-traps. "You step where I step," he says. He knows how to use the roots of trees like stairs, without ever slipping. Jose would say, "Always look for the higher ground."

One day he says, "Marsh, you are a good person."

"Really?"

"Some people are bad. You are not bad."

I say, "Thanks, I needed that."

I feel like a heel.

Walking in Circles

"Take ten," Lieutenant Heller says.

I lean against a massive tree, too weak to slap another mosquito. Andy fumbles with his medical bag, cursing as he does a hundred times a day. "That Lyndon Baines Johnson, he ought to be out here."

I say, "Andy, you crack me up." The triple canopy foliage blocks out any vestige of sun. I glance to my left and see what appears to be a work of art. Someone has carved an Army unit insignia into the tree, a Big Red One to perfection: an exact replica. "Andy, look."

He looks but doesn't say anything. Andy has only one opinion in life, maybe two: the president, and beer. "A cold beer will fix everything," he'd say.

I stare at the carving and wonder what type of character would have the ability, much less the energy, to create a miniature masterpiece in the middle of a mangrove.

Soon we move out, sloshing through unbearable mud and heat. I feel as if we're walking in a vast greenhouse with the oxygen sucked out. I imagine we're on a stage, like the old B-grade jungle movies: same props, different camera angles, fake foliage. The Vietnam War a charade.

Sundown comes, and we set up ambush on a river. Even Andy is quiet as the night passes.

The next morning we move out again with a promise of proper orientation to the map.

Halfway through the patrol we cover two thousand meters. Heller says, "Take ten."

I plop down in the soft mud and lie back on my rucksack. Andy sits too, mumbling about a cold one, and LBJ. I look up and so help me, I think I'll scream. There on the tree in front of me is the Big Red One. I leap to my feet and look around.

"Andy, we came back to the same spot. We walked in a big circle."

He looks. Cold silence.

I show Lieutenant Heller. "Look here, tell him Andy."

Andy says, "That Westmoreland, he ought to be out here."

Heller says, "We'll call for a marking round."

I hate those Willy Peters, the white phosphorous air bursts. I think the falling casing might kill me. I share my qualms with

Shireman. He says, "I know what you mean. I feel like something's gonna fall and hit me today, too."

First "Shot out!" then an air burst. Next comes the spinning hot casing falling like mini meat cleavers. I hear the casing coming down. Something says, "Move!"

I do. A piece of molten shell falls in the mud next to me. I look at the steaming six-inch hole where I once stood.

Heller finds a clearing and radios the grid coordinates to the fire base. "Should be right above our heads," he says. "Shot out!" We all gaze skyward, straining to see the popcorn-ball puff of smoke. The explosion sounds far off. One Klick downrange.

"Andy," I say, "we're walking in circles."

He says, "That McNamara. He ought to be out here. Ain't nothing a cold beer wouldn't cure right now."

Chili

"Stay five meters apart," Chili says, "one round will get us both." He slaps another mosquito, removes his steel pot, and scratches his inky black hair.

The shaded light reflects off the crossed M-60 bandoliers on his chest. Chili shifts his ammo box, turns and smiles. I see more of his back than his face.

"Watch the ants," he whispers. "Aden hit a nest."

I try to ease past the green basketball-size globe dangling above. Bright red-orange ants dive like Kamikazes. I stop for a moment to study the nest built of leaves and white glue-goop.

Keep moving.

We break for Cs. "I used to go to Elitch Park," Chili says. "They have a big wooden roller coaster there."

"I used to go to Playland," I say. "I always wanted to ride the Airplane Coaster. They tore it down the year I could finally reach the height line."

Chili tells me of his girlfriend back in Denver. "We dated in high school. I took her to the prom."

"Are you two serious?" I ask.

"We took this compatibility test," he says.

"So, are you compatible?"

"Yeah," his voice trails off. We pass a minute of silence, glancing around for movement.

Chili asks, "Do you think you'll make it back?" His dark eyes pierce mine. He's not smiling.

"I've got this feeling," I say. "I feel like I'm going to make it back."

"How do you know?"

I shrug and shake my head, picking at mud from my boot. "I believe in God."

"I believe in God too, but I don't think I'm going to make it back."

Chili's one of the kindest people I've met in all my tour. Right now he's making me uneasy. I drop the conversation; time to move out anyway.

Week after week he sloshes ahead of me. He's quiet, pensive, and compassionate. Like the day my water bladder broke again, he gave me sips of his. We trade portions of Cs.

He'll trade anything for pound cake and blackberry jam.

Chili's a year younger than me, so why does he act so much more mature?

Back on the USS Benewah, we're taking pictures with his Polaroid. He finds a way to make double exposures.

"Let's make twins," I say.

"I'm a twin," he says, "Did you know that?"

Chili uses up a roll, then hands me a few photos to keep. His olive skin and almond eyes give him a Mexican movie star look.

"I don't think I'll make it home," he says. "But I don't want anyone to cry for me."

There he goes again.

There's talk of moving to another area.

Chili starts a conversation with GoGo. I take their picture.

I try to forget the shadow on my soul, sliding over me like a silky black sheet. I feel like someone is unzipping a body bag in front of me.

I try to convince myself that someday I'll go to Elitch Park with Chili.

Take a roller coaster ride.

Promises to Keep

Aden stops cutting point long enough to radio back, "Victor Charlie!"

The Lieutenant answers, "Say again?"

"Victor Charlie!"

"Would you please say what you want to say? Jeez."

"Viet Cong, Sir. A squad of them."

"Everyone on line!" Lieutenant shouts.

We move up to Aden's position with safeties off. He recounts his tale. "I almost bumped into them."

"Well, why didn't you shoot?" Lieutenant asks.

"My weapon was slung. I couldn't get it off. They ran when they saw me."

Our platoon lies down, preparing to fire. I have problems though. GoGo Gros had given me chili salt to shake on my C-Rations. Big mistake. I used too much. Now my diarrhea is so bad that I have to keep dropping back to squat. I'm afraid the VC will come from behind and ambush me.

To compound the issue, I am cutting four wisdom teeth. With it comes a fever and malaise. I've dropped over forty pounds in the last few months. I lie down next to Chili Saiz, doubled up in pain.

"Open fire!" Heller calls. Spent shells from the M-60 bounce off my helmet. I curl up in a ball, ignoring the mayhem. Forget Charlie, I have my own war waging.

"Cease fire!" Heller yells. We advance, following little footprints that lead to their base camp. The air smells of gun powder and Nuoc Mong, the nasty fish oil.

"Their rice is still steaming on the fire," Befort says.

To our right, a camouflaged bamboo barn conceals rice. Lots of it. From the floor to the ceiling, rice. One soldier estimates fifty-seven tons.

I say, "Lieutenant, I could blow it up."

Heller says, "No, we'll have to bag it up."

As the sun sets, word trickles down that they'll be back for their food supply. "Enough to feed a whole battalion," Befort says.

Heller radios the base, "Can't you get us out? We might get pinned down here."

Command says, "Too late. Sit on it. We'll get you out tomorrow."

That night I figure it will be my last. I spread out my poncho. On it I place my .45 with clips, my grenade launcher, and bandoliers. In my pocket near my heart I keep my wooden box of twenty blasting caps. Then I pray. *Lord, please let me live. If you do, I'll be a priest, a minister, a monk, a missionary. I promise.*

Throughout the night men keep in contact with Sit Reps.

At sunrise, I sense renewed hope. Nothing's happened.

Men bag rice all day. Lieutenant says, "A general is coming out to see the cache; when he stands in front of you, salute."

The general has stars on his cap and lapels. He approaches each man on his way to the helicopter. When he comes to me he asks, "What do you want, son?"

"Sir, I just want to go home."

Then he comes to Andy. "What do you want, son?"

"Ain't nothin' a cold beer couldn't cure right now."

The general clears his throat and says, "Well," and moves on to the chopper.

Sprague Says No

We set up for the night in groups of three, away from the river bank. Dry for once.

"Another platoon is about fifty meters to our left," Bayles says.

"I didn't know they were there," I answer. The thick elephant grass and hefty trees muffle sounds.

Before sunset, their platoon receives fire. The Ninth firebase erupts with round of artillery like a chunk of volcanic rock falling. Our radio crackles a request for help. The rounds land in front of them, sending dirt and shrapnel on their own. Smoke drifts our way, and I think of firecrackers on the Fourth of July.

Another round falls. I hear yelling, commotion, confusion.

"Sergeant Sprague is over there," I say.

"He's been jumpy lately," McGee says, readjusting his helmet as we lie prone in dirt.

The lieutenant jumps up and says, "He's calling in rounds on himself."

Another round hits.

Lieutenant grabs the handset and shouts, "Cease fire! Cease fire!" He turns and says, "He should have said, *say again*. Let's get over there and help."

We crunch through brush toward the noise.

A medic tends a wounded man's leg.

I find Sprague. He's shaking, his fingers scratched and bleeding. He takes a long drag on his Camel, hands trembling.

"What happened to you?" I ask.

"I was face down and put my hands over my head like this." He demonstrates like a fieldtrip teacher. "The shell hit right there." He points to a long, V-shaped trench made by the short round. The ground is overturned, like a farmer has plowed a deep, short row and quit.

Sprague says, "I'm not coming out here again. That's it. I've got a wife and kids."

What could Engineer Sergeant Jackson say?

He won't go out either.

Unraveling

What Frightens You?

The Lieutenant calls out, "Take ten!" I lean against a sturdy mangrove tree, chatting with Andy. I try to get beyond the usual cold beer and politicians. For once he gives me his methodology of how to get out of Vietnam. "If you re-enlist for three years," he says, "you can get Germany."

"Well," I answer, "what if you do a year in Germany and then they send you back over here?"

All at once, Andy glances to his right, spins, and runs bent over like a sprinter coming out of the blocks. He struggles to snap a round in the chamber of his M-16, sliding his right hand back and forth frantically.

"Andy, where are you going" I ask, stepping forward to catch up with him.

In a split second, a large, hairy, black beast with tusks rams my left leg, spinning me clockwise 360 degrees.

"Whoa!' I yell. The animal bounds to my right, crashes though brush, then disappears as quickly as he came.

I hear Chili yell, "Look out!" The boar shakes the ground stampeding towards the right column. I hear screams and bamboo breaking. Tucker unloads a magazine, knocking it down.

Heller goes bananas. "Why did you shoot it? Don't you know these people raise them to eat?"

Another day we walk in two files. Again, the ground begins to shake like an earthquake, a 4.0 on the Richter scale. Aden calls, "Watch out!" Louder and louder the tromping grows.

I grab Chili by his rucksack and hide behind him, a human shield. A crazed, stampeding water buffalo runs past as I shove Chili in front of me. Chili slings his left fist in a roundhouse, catching me in the jaw, knocking some sense into me.

"Why did you do that?" he snaps.

"I don't know. I got scared. Sorry."

Later, Shireman tells me the graphic story of how a guy named Thompson was recently gored by a water buffalo. He says, "I thought for sure it was going to get me."

"Yeah, I know what you mean," I say.

Perhaps it is the sum total of everything.

Boars.
Booby-traps.
Red ants.
Red Alerts.
Enemy fire.
Friendly fire.
Incoming rounds.
Outgoing jets.

Nothing left to the imagination.

Frozen in the Jungle

I stare at the camouflaged bamboo table with an assortment of rockets and mortars spread out like a buffet in an all-you-can-eat restaurant. I place C-4 with a blasting cap atop the pile, an easy secondary explosion.

Afterwards, Ken Wiley and I sit talking. His smile, like many of the California guys, is genuine. He's calm, engaging, not like the paranoid New Yorkers.

April Fools Day, and we sit in the mud chatting. I say, "That was the loudest explosion I ever heard." Ken makes me feel as if I had known him all my life. Unlike most of us, Ken has a wife back home. I listen to him talk of a place called the San Fernando Valley.

In a few minutes, Wiley ferries me across a wide river, smiling in the rubber raft as if we were in a canoe on Lake Tahoe. Bill Wolters stands on shore, Instamatic in hand, snapping our picture.

The point man finds a camouflaged Chinese hand grenade on the boar trail. Too conspicuous. "This looks like a decoy," Lieutenant Heller says, "Wiley, take your squad and clover leaf out there." He points to the right of the trail where thick brush swallows them. Dones is tired, so Wiley says he'll lead.

I study the booby-traps with Hoy, Nitzel, and Befort. Hoy says, "I want a souvenir."

"I'm supposed to blow them up," I say.

Befort begins to unscrew the blasting cap.

"Wait," I say, "give me a minute to walk away."

I hurry back to the river's edge and find Kendrick and Andy mumbling.

Just then, an explosion rips the silence. In that moment, the river stops flowing, the leaves cease moving, the sun stands still. My heart quits beating.

"God!" The uncanny scream cuts the quiet. Terror fills the air.

"God!" Wiley's agonizing voice shreds my soul. It seems like an endless cry, like Mario Lanza holding the last note till his face turns blue. The hair on my neck stands up.

I hear Heller shout, "What happened?"

Wiley screams again. I scratch for cover, thinking we're under attack. To my right, Andy fumbles with his medic bag. He zips it and unzips it. Zip it open. Zip it closed.

Heller hollers, "Get the medic over here!" Andy's hands shake.

I still don't move, knowing booby-traps will be elsewhere in the thick jungle. I have become a piece of igneous rock.

To my left, Sergeant Befort marches, shouting, "I'm coming! Hold on! Andy, come on! Follow me."

My mouth drops open. Befort is walking towards them.

"Cut a landing zone," he says. "Radio, call for a Dust Off."

Wiley's voice turns to a dry, crackled moan as Andy fills him with Morphine.

Whatever self-image of bravado I held until this moment vanishes. My ego has shrunken to the size of a molecule.

I am an electron, an atom.

Lieutenant Heller Scores a Hit

The platoon sets up on the third night out along a branch of a brown river, somewhere in the uninhabitable mangrove. Free-fire zone.

The goal seems simple: wait in the dark until an enemy sampan or larger boat floats by. There should be no civilians in this 400-square-mile swamp.

Near midnight, I hear the whispered message radioed from the perimeter, "I hear a boat coming." There is no moon. I can't see my hand in front of me.

Lieutenant Heller radios estimated grid coordinates to the Fire Base, requesting artillery.

I hear the distinct sound of an artillery round approaching. The first shot plops in the water, a near miss. Too close for comfort.

Heller calls, "Drop twenty-five. Repeat."

Shot out. Artillery sounds like a hundred pigeons flapping on take off. The descent reminds me of the sound the wind makes in the elevator shaft in my apartment.

The second round scores a direct hit. KABOOM!

I bury my face in the mud. The blast feels like Hiroshima. Pieces of wood are falling. Human cells are falling. Meteorites are falling. The sky is falling.

Lieutenant Heller radios back, "Direct hit, ten KIA." He radios once more. "I say again, ten killed."

Lieutenant Heller has the reputation of being able to call in artillery rounds and put them on a dime. "Sometimes he thinks the dimes," says Bill Wolters, "are in our pockets."

Standing Guard

We're having a Protestant service," the tall chaplain with puppy-dog eyes says. "We'll meet in this clearing." He points to an open spot where shafts of light bathe the jungle. A handful of men from the 3rd/39th Infantry follow him like sheep.

I give him the once-over. No weapon.

The Catholic Chaplain, Aloysius P. McGonigal, wears a shoulder holster with a pistol, but not this Chaplain. His clear brown eyes sparkle with gentleness.

I'm no Protestant, yet I feel drawn. So I approach him. "Can I stand guard for you?"

"Why, yes," he says. "That would be nice."

I ease back against the tree and stare out to the tree line. In the early morning, the humidity rises along with my attitude.

The Chaplain begins, "You might feel angry out here."

Yeah, I'm angry. I didn't ask to leave the 4th/47th.

"You might even feel all alone."

I don't even know these men.

"You may feel frustrated."

They made so much noise last night that Pfc. Friend and I had to move off to the side.

"Your complaints may be valid."

Some lit matches and clowned. I thought we'd be hit. Yesterday that captain was doing the backstroke in the river, spitting up water like he was in the City Pool. Then he climbs ashore and shushes everyone.

The Chaplain speaks of peace. "Let go of resentment," he says. "Let it all go."

Then that captain said we're not going back in three days. We're staying out six. He acts like a nut. Let it go?

The Chaplain talks of true bonding. "You can have a real friend out here."

An unusual quiet spreads over the area, like someone has pulled a thin, cool sheet over the lush scene.

The band of men begins singing a hymn they all seem to know by heart. What is it? One I have never heard.

Have we trials and temptations?
Is there trouble anywhere?
All because we do not carry
Everything to God in prayer.
What a friend we have in Jesus,
all our sins and grief to bear.

The singing spins silk chords around me. Rays of light sneak through the tall trees. The air saturates with milky calm. I sit still, scarcely breathing. My arm cradles the barrel of my M-16, thankful that I, too, have a friend, one who sticks closer than a brother.

Cutting the Cords of Claustrophobia

Red Alert! Red Alert!" the night sergeant drones, piercing the heavy air. "Everybody get to your holes!"

I bolt upright. Outside my tent, blurry figures run like a surreal dream. *Have the VC broken in?* I scramble for my steel pot, weapon, and flack vest, adrenaline flowing.

When I reach the hole, I freeze. The life-long demon of claustrophobia raises its ugly head, threatening me.

"Get moving," someone behind me says. I jump into the darkness. *I'll crawl to the other opening to get air.* Halfway down, Bam! My helmet rams another steel pot.

"Who are you?" I ask.

"Wallace, second squad."

"What are you doing in our hole?"

"Ours is not finished yet. The Sarge told us to get in yours."

The forty-foot tunnel fills with hot bodies. I plop in the middle, trying to catch my breath. My knees touch the knees of the guy across from me. The steel plank and sandbag roof that promise protection from mortars now will be my tomb.

The press becomes unbearable. Palms sweating, I wipe them on my bunched-up flack jacket, heart racing. "I'm choking!" I shout.

The crisscross grenade bandoliers squeeze my throat in a strangle-hold. The hole smells like a locker room after Friday's practice.

"I've got to get air!" I scream. I bolt like a crazed gorilla, running bent over, stepping on arms, legs, and feet. I run amok.

"Hey!" men holler. "Ow! What are you doing?"

"Watch out!" I shout.

I arrive at the opening, gasping.

Sergeant Green stands with his back to me, waving his arms, oblivious to what I've done.

"Kendrick," he says. "Get in here."

I strain to see the silhouette standing out in the open.

"I'll take my chances out here, Sarge," Kendrick says, his arms resting on his belt gear.

"But you'll be killed! Come in!"

"Can't Sarge."

"Why not?"

"I've got claustrophobia." Kendrick shifts his weight as if he was waiting for a bus on a corner in Hartford.

I almost join the plea. But who am I to talk? I'd just stepped on nine fellow soldiers.

The next day, men come up to me lifting their fatigue shirts. "Hey, Marsh, you kicked me in the side. What happened?"

What can I say? Sorry, I just went crazy? How can I explain the fear when I don't understand it myself?

That afternoon a strange thought falls out of nowhere, like a coin dropped in a slot that falls from my head to my heart. *The next Red Alert, go to the same spot.*

I brush it off.

That night, the Sarge awakens us again. "Red Alert! Red Alert! Get to your holes."

Again, the panic. Unlaced boots slosh through muck. I arrive at the hole first, fumbling with my gear.

Go to the same spot.

Down I jump. I crawl like a crab to the exact spot in the middle and sit in the soft mud. The same crowd presses in from both ends. I feel my heart in my mouth. Sweat beads on my upper lip. I hear the guys whisper, "Where's Marsh?"

Just when I'm ready to panic, a still, small voice inside speaks: *You are the most self-centered person who ever lived.*

Like a train hissing to a station, my life comes to a halt. The brakes screech. Time stops.

Do you think the others in this hole like to be here?

I listen to the voices around me, panting, breathing heavy. Across from me sits Earl Waddell. His still misses his wife. Still unable to eat.

Next to him, Fred Silkey. Bad feet. To his left, Jimmie Wade of North Carolina. Had a hard time growing up. Nice fellow.

Down the line I scan, considering each life, their hurts, fears, wants, and needs.

Then another thought comes: *Do the loving thing.*

What would a loving thing be? I can't think of one.

Humor them.

I'm not a comic. Perhaps too serious. Melancholy.

I say, "Does anybody know what time the next bus arrives?"

Waddell answers, "Yeah, in six months."

That gets the men laughing.

"I've got a one-way ticket," Silkey says. Others chip in with corny jokes.

For the next twenty minutes the mood in the tunnel turns into a hilarious display of one-upmanship.

Hiding in a dark, wet tunnel in Vietnam, something binding lifts from me as invisible shackles fall to the muddy floor.

And for a moment, my friends and I are free.

Buddy Atwood

The cerulean sky dotted with cumulus clouds frames a perfect backdrop for the friendly figure approaching. I'd know Buddy Atwood's walk anywhere, Adonis in the Asian sun. I hop off the sandbag wall and shout, "Hey, Buddy! Where have you been?"

Atwood is all Bronx, the ideal Buck. When I joined his platoon in early March, he stepped up to extend a firm grip and say-hey smile. In May, I got pulled back to Bearcat and haven't seen him in a month.

"Hey, Marshy, they're dead."

"What? Who's dead?"

"Jimmy Burroughs, Henke, Chili—"

"Chili?" I shove my hands deep into my fatigue pockets and try to catch my breath. Atwood keeps talking, but his voice sounds like a radio fading in and out. The helicopter pad behind my tent drones an endless hum of rotor blades slapping humid air. The whirr spins my head.

"I can't believe it," I say. "Not Chili. What happened?" *Ronald J. Saiz gone?*

"I missed the patrol," Atwood says. "I'd been in the hospital in Long Binh with an infected leg. Marshy, I was pulling the dead and wounded off the choppers."

Atwood's lips continue to move but I only catch bits and pieces.

"Lieutenant got part of his face blown off—Sergeant Jones lost an arm and may not make it—Chili got hit right in the heart—"

My mind is reeling. I feel like screaming, like running, like shooting somebody.

Atwood recounts the story, "Chili said, 'Charlie, hold my hand.' Charlie Zies told me that Chili shook once and died."

Atwood says something about the medic running out of Morphine, but my thoughts are stuck in park, emergency brake on.

I stare beyond the perimeter. *I'll get those Viet Cong. They'll pay for this.*

"I want to go back out there," I say, clenching my teeth. "I want to get even." I feel like a Coke bottle, shaken and ready to burst.

"What good would that do?" Fox turns and walks away. A transistor radio in a nearby tent blares a Sonny and Cher song: "The beat goes on. Drums keep pounding rhythm to the brain."

I'm hyperventilating and my nose flares.

I lean against the sandbag wall and glance at Atwood broadcasting bad news. Each word, like a mason's trowel, seals my heart with cement, layer upon layer.

In the distance, the muffled artillery pounds, more to be killed.

I vow to get back out there, to the 4th/47th.

I'll get even.

Atwood and I shake hands, and he walks out of my life.

Top Sergeant

Top Sergeant never asks, "What are you doing?" Instead he asks, "What are you supposed to be doing?" The Prince of Intimidation.

When our company stood in formation the first day at Ft. Riley, he said, "I will inspect you every morning."

Everyone groaned.

Then he said, "I have nine children. I line them up every morning before school. I walk down the line while they stand at attention. I check out their hair, their clothes, their shoes. Even behind the ears." No one doubted him.

To say that Top runs a tight ship is an understatement.

Rules are spelled out clearly. There will be no socializing with, or speaking to, any Vietnamese. Agreed. There will be no alcohol, no drugs, no rebellion.

Pfc. Jimmie D. Inman, a joker from Charlotte, does a perfect impression of Top. "Rimmer," he says, "What are you SUPPOSED to be doing?" "Were you THINKING of talking with that Vietnamese?" Inman has everyone rolling.

Inman has a dark side, too. At Ft. Riley I heard him say, "If there's one thing I hate, it's an uppity nigger."

His buddy, Pfc. Williams, nodded.

When the phrase, "Afro-American" came out, Inman would ask, "Are you Afro?" He turned it into a racial slur: "Afro?"

August arrives and it's time for Top to rotate back to the States. The company chips in and buys him a gold watch. During the goodbye service, I sit next to Inman.

Top begins his speech, "Thank you for the very nice watch. I have put all I had into protecting all of you."

Everyone nods.

"But I am leaving here a failure," he says. A few gasps could be heard around the room. I glance at Inman. He, too, looks puzzled.

"I have failed because of the needless death of Pfc. Williams. I take full responsibility for Williams' death." Top walks away from the podium and sits.

The room erupts into a thunderous standing ovation. Inman blinks back tears.

Later I ask Jimmie Inman, "Why did you clap? I thought you hated Black people."

"Top is a man," he says. "He is a real man."

Welcome New Top

The day after Top leaves, the new guy arrives. He calls a formation. Some of the company is still out on patrol. He announces, "We will cancel formations." He slouches, looks sleepy. "We'll have them only when I feel we need them."

A few cheer, but most keep quiet. I feel as if a dance has ended and the band is packing up for the night.

"We will also arrange for beer," he continues. "We'll have plenty."

A few applaud. I glance at McGee. He's shaking his head.

The next day stacks of canned beer arrive on pallets. The new Top swings his arms directing the loader. He's chain smoking.

A month later he calls the only other formation I can remember. He is hung over and his uniform wrinkled.

"I have here a Good Conduct Medal for Robert Bayly," he says. "He's rotating back to the States."

Bayly marches to the front and gives a salute. Top doesn't see it.

Bayly, like a good soldier, stands at attention.

He holds his salute while Top pins the medal on him.

Learning the Hard Way

Schook's platoon moves back to Dong Tam in May. Funny how I missed hearing his mouth these past three months.

On August 8th, word comes out of Qiang Ngai Province. Something has happened.

Sergeant Schook was riding on the front fender of a jeep, as he often did. Louis Prunty was sweeping the road, careful about what he was hearing. Vito was nearby.

"Prunty," Schook said, "you're going too slow. Speed it up."

Prunty said, "I'm hearing metal in the road, Sarge."

Schook said, "Give me that thing and get out of the way."

The jeep bumped along with Sergeant Schook waving his mine detector back and forth in a fast-acting motion, spitting and talking to the driver. The right front wheel hit an anti-tank mine. Schook and the driver were killed.

That evening as we stand around outside the tents, MacIntosh says, "I just can't believe it. Of all people, not Sergeant Schook."

I say, "How could it happen? How could he let it happen?"

His death doesn't make sense in a war that makes no sense.

The Visit

In August, 1967, I am back at Bearcat. My cot is temporarily moved to a sergeant's tent. The new Top stays at the end, near the flap, hoping to catch the first breeze before it plays out. Top likes his beer and girlie books.

One evening, a man comes through to spend the night. He wears pressed green fatigues, no name tag, no insignia. His short, gray hair has a silver tint. His eyes are the shade of blue steel. He stands six feet two, aristocratic, soft-spoken. He emits a quiet assurance.

The man neither smokes nor drinks. He doesn't join in with the other sergeants' foolish talk.

We speak of life in general. I am drawn to his silent aura.

That night on the cot next to mine he says, "America cannot win this war."

I say, "Really? How do you know?"

"Trust me, I know."

"What outfit do you work with?" I ask.

"Oh," he says hesitating, "let's just say, Intelligence."

"When will it end?" I ask.

"Five years or so. A few more." He speaks with calm tones. I feel as though I have known him for a long time. We talk into the night.

The next morning, his cot is empty. I never see him again.

Radio Holding

Efren Ruiz bends, filling sandbags next to Pfc. Holding of Fort Worth. Holding shows Ruiz photos of his platinum hair that wowed the girls back in Texas. He's bleached, tanned, and grinning like a wild boy with no boundaries.

Holding says, "They called me Sonny. That was my nickname."

Ruiz says, "Sony? That's a radio."

From that day on, Holding is known as Radio.

Several nights Radio wakes up screaming "God! No! God!" making the hair on everyone's neck stand up. Radio says, "Oh, God, I had a bad dream. I was dying."

His buddy, Pfc. Heckman from New Jersey, says, "He's nuts. I think he took too much dope."

Radio has a hideous laugh and often spouts the intellectual benefits of drugs. One day he is sitting on the ground talking with Lionel MacKenzie. Heckman says, "Will you look at that. Just look at the two of them. Now that's a pair." MacKenzie talks philosophy while Radio sits grinning.

One day, Radio disappears. I mean, vanishes. "He's not to be found," Heckman says. "I think he's AWOL. I'll bet he ran off with one of them mama-sans."

Jimmie Wade writes My-Lan, the DJ on the Armed Forces radio. Over the next few days she says, "Will Sonny Radio Holding please return to your company."

Radio never returns.

Sleeping Sickness

Sergeant Shultz scratches his balding head and yawns, squinting as he closes the tent flap behind him. "What time is it?" he asks.

"You're a little late for breakfast," MacIntosh says, "It's almost noon."

How did Shultz become an E6? One day he shows up in our 15th Engineer outfit, laughing at everything. His bad habit stands out like a white suit in a junk yard. He sleeps all the time. When he's awake, he walks around with his eyelids at half-mast.

MacIntosh says, "I wonder if this guy's got the sleeping sickness."

Bodner, the company trivia expert says, "No, that's from a mosquito in Africa."

Soon, Shultz gets a package containing a primitive record player in a small case with a broken handle. Problem is, no records. MacIntosh loans him an album by The Mamas and the Papas. Sergeant Shultz hears the song "Monday, Monday" and says, "Ooh, I like that. I like it a lot. Can I play it again?"

"Sure," Mac says.

The next day, Shultz is discovered on his cot, with "Monday, Monday" on replay.

When he awakens, he laughs and says, "What day is it?"

One morning Shultz says, "The Top is sending me to see the psychiatrist."

No one seems surprised.

Late that afternoon, Shultz returns to the company area. Mac says, "Hey Sarge, what did they do to you?"

"Well, the doctor told me to relax. He said to lie down on a couch to talk."

"Yes?"

"So I fell asleep. I don't know what he said."

The next day, Sergeant Shultz is shipped out, a set of orders, the record player, and The Mamas and Papas album tucked safely beneath his arm.

He grins and waves as he goes.

Coke War

"Riots are breaking out in some cities back home," Tom Smith says. His eyes are a deep, chocolate brown, his skin the color of coffee, no cream.

"Really?" I say.

Smitty and I first got to know each other better when we shared a foxhole for two weeks in February. We spent more time together in

Smith has a history. He got into an argument with the law in Youngstown. The police told him to move along. Smith said, "I live here. These are my front steps." The scene turned physical. A court appearance followed. The judge gave a choice: go to jail or join the Army. Smitty made his choice. Somewhere along the line he straightened up and became a good soldier.

Smith says, "Marshy, they're threatening not to serve Blacks at the Coke tent."

"What?"

"Will you come with me and get a Coke?"

"I'll buy," I say. We ask some other Whites if they'll join us. No one moves. I can see their point. No sense looking to create trouble. Why cause a riot here?

The Coke tent stands next to the mess hall. Along the way I say, "Smitty, do you remember when you dropped me back into the water when I tried to stay dry? I've got a good mind to let you go in there alone."

"Yeah, but that big snake was slithering over my boots. I had to let you go."

"I forgive you," I say.

I enter the Coke tent first. Some soldiers from Carolina and Georgia stand behind the counter. I recognize them from A Company.

"Who's your friend?" one asks.

"You know Tom Smith," I say. "We just got back from the field. It was rough out there. I'd like two Cokes." I place the money down and smile.

He looks at me.

I stare at him.

The fellow slams the two cans on the wooden counter. "Here," he says.

"Thanks."

"Here you go, Smitty." I hand him a Coke.

Smith puts his arm on my shoulder as we walk out into the humid night.

There's fighting in Vietnam. There's fighting in Detroit. And there's fighting over a Coke.

Exposed

Unarmed

Red Alert! Red Alert!" the night sergeant cries, stirring me awake.

I fumble with my gear and take my time heading for the hole, arriving last. I hop down into the dark opening, already abuzz with complaining. One more GI follows me. Ronald Seigford.

"Great," I mutter.

The air already reeks with the stench of hot, sweaty bodies. Sergeant Green squats to my right and gives me an order. "Sergeant Marsh, find somebody to get the ammo."

The ammo is stored in a sandbagged area about fifty meters away. I turn to the only man on my left and say, "Seigford, go get the ammo."

Pfc. Seigford is a Lifer. He's built like a nose guard, 210 pounds of beef. A scar runs from near his right eye to his mouth. "A guy cut me with a bottle during a bar fight in Alaska," he once told me.

Top had Seigford transferred to Graves Registration. They sent him back after one month. He'd irritate everyone with his psychotic breaks and cryptic conversation. "Lai Kai. Dead bodies," he said, eyes glazed. Just this week I saw him standing at the perimeter holding up a bandolier, speaking to no one. "Look, Charlie," he said, "I've got grenades. I'm warning you."

The Top had to take away his weapon.

I turn to Seigford and repeat the order. He doesn't move. He says, "I got it last week."

"Go get the ammo!" I shout.

"I'm not going out there. Get somebody else."

I lose it. I turn to Seigford and scream, "Go get the ammo now!"

"I got it last week," he says. "Get someone else."

My mind cracks open like a fresh egg. Before I can stop myself I point my M-16 at his heart and snap a round in the chamber. With my right thumb, I click the safety off. My index finger rests firmly on the trigger. Beads of sweat pop out on my forehead. The men in the hole look on in silent disbelief. My hand shakes as I apply slight pressure on the trigger.

"You're crazy, man," Seigford says. He scurries away into the dark to run his errand.

I click the safety on, eject the round, lower the rifle, and put my head in my hands.

All the men, including my squad leader, look on. Shame pours over me like hot lead, scalding my soul.

I almost killed a confused, unarmed boy wearing a man's body.

Charge of Quarters

Charge of quarters, or CQ, means, "Stay awake all night." Part of the job is to make rounds in the company area, every hour on the hour. Make sure everyone gets woken up if there's an attack, and head off any foul play. In the morning, we awaken the mine sweepers.

That day our platoon had a small cookout for one of the men rotating back to the States. Hot dogs and Cokes, and some had too many beers. Sergeant Baker wanted a picture taken with me.

That night, Baker comes into the CQ tent. He snoops around, loitering for no apparent reason. I check the clock. 2 a.m.

I ask, "What do you want?"

"Oh," he says, "I'm tired." He sits down next to me at the desk. "Can I lay my head down right here?" With that he tries to lay his head on my right thigh.

I had heard he tried the same thing with Pfc. Ambiotti.

"No, you can't. Leave now."

I stand facing him. My fists curl. I don't care that he is an E7 or six feet two. "I don't play. Beat it."

He turns and walks out into the darkness.

In my pocket is a wallet with my Army ID and a Bible verse I cut out a year ago. It reads, "Eye hath not seen, neither ear heard, nor has entered into the heart of man the things that God hath prepared for those that love him."

On the CQ desk sits a transistor radio. I flip on the radio knob. The newscaster announces, "The St. Louis Cardinals just won the World Series!"

World Series? Are people really playing baseball?

Drainage

Drainage! Man your shovels!" Jackson's voice booms above the pelting monsoon wash. Muck and mud become our new enemy.

We sling our weapons and grab long-handle shovels, trudging ankle deep in Laterite. With dark clouds come a dark mood, like an agitated python slithering through the company area..

I wish I could be out on patrol with the 4th/47th. Not here with these stupid shovels.

About fifty meters down the road I notice Hannold, a blond Hercules from Ohio. His arms flail as he banters with Cool Jerk, his squad leader aptly named after a popular tune.

I think back to training. I had watched Hannold fashioning a foxhole, slamming his entrenching tool into the Kansas dirt. Cool Jerk sat nearby napping, his head bobbing like a helium balloon, his uniform wrinkled. Saliva dripped from his dangling lower lip.

Hannold's mouth got him in hot water. "Look at him," he said, "that sorry Lifer, hiding in the Army. He couldn't make it on the outside."

Now I can see Hannold again ready to explode like a pressure cooker under high heat. He jams the shovel into the mud and squares off with Cool Jerk.

I turn back to my own shovel as I chop a small gully and watch the water find its way towards the waiting ditch.

"Eight months training," I say to Bayles, "nine months in country, and what are we doing? Drainage."

I glance back at Hannold.

C'mon Hannold, what are you waiting for? Hit the Jerk.

What's Wrong with Me?

Sergeant Baker calls me into a vacant tent. I have my guard up. He'd better not try anything.

I glance around. Twenty chairs are lined up in a classroom-like setting. A make-shift wooden podium leans forward, like it is tired from the heat.

"I want you to speak," he says. "There're some green troops coming tomorrow. I want you to teach a class about booby-traps."

"No, I don't want to."

"But you can save lives," Baker says, leaning forward on his chair, his mouth hanging open.

"I can't speak in front of people."

Baker asks me to stand at the podium. I do.

"Talk," he says. "Tell me about Operation Greenleaf."

"I can't, and I won't."

Back and forth we banter until Baker's Cheshire cat grin turns to a scowl. He swishes out, slapping back the canvas flap.

I am still fuming about his inappropriate advances.

What's wrong with me? Why won't I help new recruits?

Freddie

Efren Ruiz-Galarza sways by his bunk singing, "Oigua me madre aun…"

I ask, "What does that mean?"

"I can still hear my mother. In the song she's calling me."

Ruiz would mambo through the barracks in Fort Leonard Wood. With smooth moves he'd say, "Salsa, Marsh."

His almond eyes are riveting, shining like black pieces of onyx. He sports a half-smile, with a slight tilt of the head, as if straining to understand every word. I listen to his sagas about Puerto Rico, the white beaches of Ponce, and often, he'll talk of his mother.

Ruiz picked up the nickname Freddie and would samba the summer away during our training at Fort Riley, right up to boarding ship in September.

In Vietnam, Freddie doesn't go on many patrols. Instead, Sergeant Jackson finds him "projects" to do on Bearcat. Nobody minds.

Months roll by.

One week in late August, I'm assigned a detail with Freddie attached. "Build an obstacle course of booby-traps," Jackson says, "for the new recruits."

"Here, Ruiz," I say. "Carry these pieces of bamboo." We fabricate a genuine Punji pit, stakes and all. Next we fashion a pickle can with spikes in it, pointing downward. "Help me get this in the hole," I say. "If anybody steps in it, the natural instinct would be to pull the foot out." The spikes would enter the leg at the tibial area.

Each day, Freddie grows quieter. We make swinging things, boards with nails, and contraptions that would win "Show and Tell" in any Viet Cong classroom.

One afternoon, Freddie quits singing. No more smiles. No dancing.

I say, "We've got to finish this today."

"I want to go home," Ruiz says. "I'm tired of this. Not much time left over here. I'm short."

After eleven months in country, the tour is sapping him, like an invisible force sucking the spirit away, leaving an empty shell.

But I don't care.

I say, "Freddie, let's get busy. We've got a deadline."

He sits on a stump and says, "I'm not working anymore."

"You have to work," I say, "I'm in charge and we have to finish."

"No, I'm finished."

I face Ruiz. He stands, appearing more like a lamb than a lion. His black eyebrows furrow. He looks quizzical, like a scolded boy about to cry.

But I keep on. I am a caldron, cast iron, churning like witch's brew bubbling over fire.

"If you don't get busy," I say, "I'm going to punch you right in the nose." I feel my fist ball up, trembling. My breathing grows rapid. "I said get busy."

Freddie offers me a half-smile and pierces me with onyx eyes. He is dying, and all I care about is the project.

"I want to go home," Freddie says. "I want to see my mother."

Dead Serious

Sergeant Sprague stands staring at the mosquito net shrouding his cot.

"What are you looking at?" I ask.

He doesn't answer. Maybe he sees burn holes made from cigarettes that angry men do in passing to agitate those not well liked. I have a few myself.

No, Sprague is nice. Everybody likes the jovial guy from Maine.

"Sprague," I say, "what are you doing?"

He turns. His face is pale, his eyes wide. He looks like he wants to be far away, in the piney woods north of Bangor. I walk over to him. "What's the matter?"

Rex points to a small metal object lying atop his mosquito net. A hand grenade ring and pin in plain sight. I try to process what malicious intent the message sends.

"Who would put that there?" I ask.

"That's what I want to know. Somebody's out to frag me."

"Do you think it's because you refused to go out anymore?"

"Could be, but I don't care. I am not going out anymore. I'm short. I got kids."

He is serious. Dead serious.

A Short Trip to Tan Tru

"Hey, I've got orders for Fort Polk," I say, "tank crew."

Sergeant Gabriel's cot sits across from mine. He says, "I thought you wanted to get out when you got back."

"I do. I have three months left. I wish I could get out early. I can't see going back to spit and polish."

Gabriel, a Lifer, knows the ropes. "Just fill out a 1049," he says. "They'll drop your last three months. All you have to do is stay in Vietnam for one more month. It's an early out."

I usually pray about major decisions. Not this time.

"It's a gamble," he says.

In a week, my papers are accepted. Now all I have to do is stay on Bearcat for four weeks, kicking back and counting days.

The next day, Sergeant Jackson says, "Marsh, I have a mission for you."

I've grown to dread that word "mission."

Jackson says, "You need to take this young driver down to a place called Tan Tru. Ride shotgun. Deliver a trailer of water."

When I meet the fellow, he looks pale. It's his first trip out. We hop into his deuce and a half with a water trailer in back. No convoy, just pony express. Sounds risky. I've never been to Tan Tru.

That morning we head out, map in hand, light rain falling as we leave Bearcat. After an hour, we pass rubber plantations. I begin to get nervous.

"Step on it," I say.

I can't figure out why there is no traffic on the muddy highway. I keep staring to my left, rubber trees as far as the eye can see, lined up like endless corridors. I imagine men in black pajamas hiding behind each one.

The trailer fishtails in the mud, back and forth, sliding the width of the road. I glance at the driver, Billy, and notice beads of sweat dotting his face. He keeps his front wheels in the soft, deep ruts.

I snap a round in the chamber and flip the safety off, fingering my magazines. I glace at the ammo boxes beneath my feet.

"We have some more behind the seat," Billy says.

If we do get ambushed, who would know we're here? We have no radio. No phone.

Where is this place?

The trailer zigzags like a water skier.

Why did I sign that 1049? I could be on my way to Fort Polk right now.

The highway runs for miles; dark, looming trees bend as if to harass me, their branches like arms reaching to strangle me. The ride is like a recurring dream and I can't wake up.

At dusk we finally roll into the small base. We circle the area looking for our drop-off contact. By the time we unhitch the trailer, I know it's too late to go back.

Will we be missed? Does anyone care?

We walk over to a small stage area and catch the end of a show. The singer has a troupe with him. Someone says it's Hank Snow. I don't know how secure this camp is. I have a hard time listening.

Now I feel like Sprague and Jackson.

I don't want to come out anymore.

I'm short.

Fungus

Sergeant Gabriel is a husky Mexican-American. Each night he plays the same record album, Cuco Sanchez, *Guitarras por la Media Noche.* But after one patrol he says, "Look at my skin. I got the jungle rot."

"You're fire engine red," I say. A blotch resembling a map of the world runs from his neck to his knees. He stands in shorts, afraid to move for pain. "Where's the base doctor?" he asks.

It seems a common thing, the outbreak. Fred Silkey has it on his feet. They turn grey with scores of small craters like on the moon. Fred is confined to his cot for two weeks, up only for latrine and chow.

After one patrol I, too, get a bad rash, this one between my legs. I make the mistake of asking the chubby medic for help, the one that smothered his monkey. He says, "I'll fix you right up. I know just what you need." He hands me a cup with some brown salve. "Apply it twice a day," he says.

I walk behind a truck and smear a bit on. When I return, I say, "That stuff really burns."

"Burns?"

"Like fire." I've never had anything hurt so badly. It is like someone put a blow torch on my groin. Like scalding water poured on my genitals.

Next thing, I'm on my back in the dirt. It's as if I'm looking in the wrong end of binoculars. Then, blackness.

I wake with three men standing over me. When they pick me up, one says, "Man, your eyes rolled back in your head."

The medic says, "Ha-ha. I guess you shouldn't use that stuff again."

Two weeks later, the fungus in my ears is excruciating. With one day left in Vietnam, I visit the base doctor. He says, "To treat it, we'll have to put you in the hospital."

I say, "Doc, I'm flying home tomorrow. I want out. I'll go to my doctor in New York."

I don't care if I am bleeding or have the fungus over ninety percent of my body. I'm going home.

Finding John Boraski

The thirteen month tour in Nam seemed like thirteen years. I lost forty-two pounds and browned like a Florida surfer. While riding in a rickety bus to the airport, I see a dead Viet Cong strung up on a pole by the side of the road. I try not to look.

Earlier that day, Top approached me. He reached into his pocket and pulled out a Good Conduct Medal. "Here," he said. "I forgot to have a ceremony."

"Thanks," I said, then walked away.

The flight from Saigon to San Francisco will stop for fuel in Tokyo. With each leg of the journey comes angst. Will I find home the same? Have I changed? Will my friends be different?

Once in Oakland, we are herded to an olive drab, barred-windowed bus that speeds us to a base for a quick exit physical. No desensitization, no counseling, no debriefing.

As I step off the curb, a carload of hippies swerves, intending to hit me. I jump back when their rickety Toyota grazes my duffle bag, sending me in a 360.

Welcome home.

I dust myself off and hear a voice behind me say, "Hey, Jim."

"Boraski! What are you doing here?"

"I just got back from Vietnam."

"I did too. John, it's good to see you."

"Yeah, you too."

"How are you doing?" I ask.

"Okay."

Once inside the crowded barracks, we check plane tickets. Oakland to New York, October 17, 1967. I say, "We're on the same flight."

"Do you have a ride from the airport?" I ask.

"My wife's coming," he says.

"Can I get a lift?"

"Sure." John seems stiff.

"What are you thinking about?" I ask.

"My wife. How I'll handle it."

During the long flight home, I study Boraski. Gaunt, tanned, quieter. I notice a distance in his eyes. The plane hits a few pockets and we both grip the armrest.

Finally, the captain announces JFK lay ahead, so up go the tray tables and seats. As the plane banks hard left, I notice the wing, the water, the waves.

Then I remember. The flight over. Who we were. Who we left behind.

I glance at John. He doesn't blink or swallow. He stares out the window at nothing.

He's like a shell. Like somebody sucked the life out of him. I want him to be to the old John, to tell me he has a hand grenade, to leap from his seat and scream, "We're going to crash! Pull up!" Say anything, scream anything. Instead, we walk stone-faced to the baggage area. How I wish he'd smile, crack a joke, talk about home.

It takes me a few decades to understand what happened. Boraski was a bruised reed, bent, nearly broken. Feelings sealed in, like the alabaster jugs the Viet Cong used to store smelly fish oil. And in the mirror of his face, I saw myself.

Boraski and I are two of tens of thousands of Vietnam vets who survived a tour but died somewhere in Southeast Asia.

Jennaro Lovito

A few days after we return from overseas, a knock comes at my door. I open it and there stands John Boraski. The first thing he says is, "Do you remember Jerry Lovito?"

What kind of question is that? Of course I remember Lovito.

During Basic, Paul Munoz had said, "Hey, Lovito, you know what your name means in Spanish?"

"What does it mean?"

"Little Wolf."

Lovito lived in Port Chester and was one of the scores drafted in our batch. He, too, went to Vietnam and came back at the same time as Boraski and me.

"He was killed last night in a car wreck," Boraski says. "He was double-dating with the Arita kid and his girl. They were coming back from a movie in White Plains."

I stand there stunned.

"Lovito took his money saved from the Army and bought a new Camaro," Boraski continues. "They tried to get away from this guy who was bothering them and got off at the Purchase Exit. They were going so fast they couldn't make the curve. They hit the abutment and were killed."

I stand there in silence. I have no words.

Spend a year dodging death in Vietnam only to come home and die.

The Summer of Love

My palms are already moist when Professor Mortimer Clark scans the class to pick the first victim for an impromptu speech. Three credits are all I need to complete my Associate Degree, and Public Speaking is my last holdout.

Throughout the class I can hear the muffled coughs, the clearing of throats. Perhaps the thirty other adults feel the same as I do.

"Mister Marsh," Clark says, "come up to the front. You're first."

My legs twitch. I fight to raise my eyes. "You have one minute," he says. "Talk about anything."

"I, I can't think of anything."

"Tell us about yourself."

I stand behind the wooden podium, clutching the sides. I look up, feeling naked. "I just got back from Vietnam," I say. I stare at the grandmother on the front row, her hair in a bun. She gives a sympathetic nod. A bead of sweat forms on my upper lip. I flash back to Sergeant Baker trying to get me to speak.

"I spent some time in the jungle." My voice trails off and my throat tightens.

Clark breaks in from the back of the room. "You're turning red."

I'm sinking. Blushing always comes at the wrong times. My cheeks burn. I wipe my forehead with my sleeve and take a breath.

"Now you're turning white," he says, standing and waving his arms.

He draws a few chuckles. The old lady covers her mouth.

"Now you're turning green," Clark says as he walks to the front.

"You know, class," he says, "it's people like this that foster war, that kill innocent babies and children and cause this country to be in the mess it's in."

Is this guy serious?

His arms flail, and a fine mist of spit flies from his mouth. On he rants, now in front of the class.

I slink back to my seat and blink fast. I clench my teeth and curl my toes. I am a red, white and green no-good Vietnam vet. A woman behind me touches my back. I want to turn and thank her. Instead, I sit like a mummy, embalmed. *Stuff it all inside.*

The next few weeks are torture. I fight my way through each speech, turning colors.

One night as I bustle through the crowded halls, I see Rory O'Brian at the far end. Rory has Irish written all over his face; cobalt eyes, ruddy cheeks. His broad shoulders and bulging biceps make his shirt appear two sizes too small. He towers over everyone. Rory is five years older then me and likes my sister Roberta.

Without warning, Rory turns to a passing figure. Mortimer Clark. Rory grabs Clark's collar and knit tie with his left hand, twists it in his red, calloused vise grip, and lifts Clark off the floor.

I can't believe what I'm seeing.

Should I get involved?

Rory pins him to the painted concrete block wall and cocks his fist, ready to deliver a Limerick right cross.

Rory could really hurt him.

This could be my opportunity to be a peacemaker, to say, "Aw, Rory, leave him alone. C'mon, don't hurt him."

Another part of me dips a ladle into the hurt and pain buried in my soul's cauldron.

Don't care.

I turn my head and walk out without looking back.

All I need is three credits.

Re-Enlisting

Sergeant Bill leans forward, placing his elbows on the Oak desk. He reminds me of a kid on Christmas eager to open a present.

My hand shakes as if I've just turned ninety. I reach for the ballpoint to sign my life away. *Why am I reenlisting?*

Sergeant Bill sits back, smiling like he had a new set of bridges, and places his hands behind his head. "You won't regret this," he says.

Someone once told me that recruiters needed to enlist three a month or they will be re-assigned to the boonies. Am I number three? He reminds me of an insurance man rolling the pen to close the sale.

Outside, the sunlight glistens off the busses and cars bustling along the avenue. High noon, for sure. I tell him I want Infantry.

Without warning, an eerie darkness creeps into the room, turning my heart to ice, an instant Antarctica. Midnight in a second. I glance at Sergeant Bill. He smiles, nodding.

I lay the pen down and say, "I just remembered something I need to check."

"Oh?" he says.

"I'll be right back," I say and bolt for the door. I hop into my '65 Mustang Fastback and use every one of the 289 cubic inches on that high-performance motor to flee. I never look back.

The next day at work I share the story with Tony. Tony has recently seen dramatic changes in his life with his new-found faith. When I finish the tale, Tony says, "That's the devil."

I can't argue with him.

Sergeant Bill tracks me down by phone. "You made me do all that paperwork."

"I'm sorry," I say. "I don't know what's wrong with me. I can't go back in right now."

As I gently aim the phone toward its cradle, his hollow voice, as in a well, spews long-forgotten but familiar expletives.

Re-Up Twice

I clutch the yellow legal envelope containing my orders for Officer Candidate School, signed, sealed, and delivered. My hand trembles as I reached for the payphone and dial the recruiting office.

"Hello," the voice says, "Sergeant Bill speaking."

"Hi, this is Jim Marsh."

"Yes? And what can I do for you, Jim?"

"Sarge, I've got a problem."

"A problem?" I can tell his blood pressure is rising.

I take a deep breath and begin. "I'm out here in Dallas. I can't go into the Army."

"What?" I've pushed him to the edge of the precipice. He's about to fall off into a bottomless pit. He'll make a murder plot for me.

I've just come out of a sermon by Lane Adams at a national Christian conference. I feel convinced I shouldn't go.

"Why can't you go?" Sergeant Bill's voice is at near eighty decibels.

"I just can't. I don't know how to explain."

"But you have orders!" he screams. "You signed the papers! You made a written commitment! You have to go!"

I sense desperation, exasperation, an understandable madness, like a man stabbed in the back twice with a dull kitchen knife and left bleeding.

I pause. A quiet thought comes like a cool north wind on a muggy June day. "But Sarge," I say, "I didn't swear in yet."

He utters a loud oath, then CLICK.

My mother is a nurse in Westchester at the time. A week later I call her to tell her I'm not re-enlisting. She tells me that Bill had a heart attack and bypass surgery soon after my call.

I am a dirty, rotten heel.

Three Strikes, You're Out

I am finishing my master's degree at Springfield College in Massachusetts. The demon of guilt hounds me with whispers, "You failed God. You must go back in the Army and make up for your mistakes."

So I visit the recruiter in town. The Sarge asks, "What was your MOS?"

"11B40, Combat Engineer."

"What was your rank?"

"Buck."

"Well, what do you know," he says. "We have one slot for an E-6, Demo man. I can give you a stripe if you'll sign up."

"Okay," I say. "Do the paperwork, and I'll be back tomorrow." I feel that churning in my belly like I ate too many green apples.

The following day I visit the recruiter's office. He lays the paper in front of me. "Just sign here," he says, "and you'll be in the Reserves for six years."

A clear, quiet, commanding thought comes into my head like a bar of Ivory floating to the top of bath water. *Ask him if you can move from Springfield in the next six years.*

"Do I have to stay here in Springfield?" I ask, "or can I move back to New York?"

"No, you have to stay here in Springfield."

"Sir," I say, "I'm sorry for your time. I can't do it."

I turn away, breathing deep the fresh New England air, my tennis shoes kicking yellow-red oak leaves along the sidewalk.

When Jesus died, He died for all your mistakes.

Processing

Bill Bright

Sergeant Bill's rage echoes in my head. I feel so guilty I decide not to return to New York to face him. Some friends say, "Let's go out to California."

The thought of returning to grad school seems tiring, so I say, "Sure."

On Monday, June 19, 1972, we arrive at Arrowhead Springs in San Bernardino. "Bill Bright is speaking," my friend Richard says.

Yellow-gray smog creeps through the Chino Valley from LA like a slithering poisonous snake. Dr. Bright stands to speak in the outdoor amphitheater to two hundred or so college students. He's calm and positive, talking about Jesus and love.

Afterwards, I approach him. "You said to keep Christ on the throne of your heart. But what if you have trouble doing that?"

"Either Christ in on the throne of your heart or he isn't."

I ponder my self-centeredness. *Maybe that's it: self on the throne.*

Bright doesn't wait for a reply. "Who do you want on the throne of your life?"

The question cuts my heart like a surgical scalpel. I glance left to the valley as the smog lifts. A Santa Ana breeze kicks up. I look back at him. Dr. Bright's brown eyes sparkle like the lights in the city below.

He adds, "It's a moment-by-moment yielding of self by faith, not feelings. That is the key."

The sun hides behind the mountains to the West. I turn to the hills behind the amphitheater and notice the enormous natural arrowhead pointing downward to the place where we are standing.

Arrowhead Springs. The Indians say it is holy ground, a sacred place. I want it all to fall into place, to surrender to the yielding. But I just don't know how yet. I just don't know how.

The Dream

Ever so often since 1967, I'd have a nightmare and wake up in a heavy sweat. Sometimes I'd hear Wiley's screams even after I opened my eyes. Other times, I'd wake up feeling guilty. *Why did I live and others die?*

Then, on Tuesday, February 7, 1989, I have a dream. I am loaded with full gear, trudging through a low-lying swamp. Suddenly I see swarms of the enemy racing toward us. They are on foot and heavily armed. My companion turns and runs. I follow. I feel them closing in, even though I'm running as fast as I can. Under branches and toward a mountain I run, trying to make it to safety. I fall on my face in the mud and cry, "Oh God!" I'm consumed by impending doom and despair.

Then, just when I think I'm going to die, a strong hand touches my shoulder. A soldier lifts me up. When I turn to face the soldier I am shocked. The enemy turns out to be Americans, my friends. I walk on with them, my arm around this man's waist, thanking God, repenting for my failure, and sensing His love through the love of these caring men. Then the one walking with me speaks. "It's okay. That happens to all of us."

When I awaken, I still feel the peace.

The nightmares end for good.

Finding a Way Out

"We're going to Immanuel Church today," my wife announces.

"I don't want to go there," I say. "That's where Bill Clinton goes. It's too political."

"We have to go," she replies. "The boys went to church today with the Rainwater kids. We have to pick them up."

"I'm tired," I say. "I'm really tired."

I am a reed bent by the wind, broken. I am a rock, sunken to the bottom of a dark blue lake.

We arrive at the archaic yellow-brown building and mount the long stone stairs, past looming columns and old oak doors. The place matches my spirit.

"Let's go to the balcony," I say.

I flop onto the wooden seat, rest my feet on an empty chair back, and open the bulletin. Sunday, February 29, 1994. Henry Blackaby, Guest Speaker.

"Hey, Susie, I think I've heard of this guy."

Out walks a teddy bear of a man, perhaps ten years older than me. When he starts to talk, I sit up. I grab a pen and begin scribbling notes. "Make your heart a highway over which Jesus Christ can walk," he says.

I feel a stirring, as if a lock falls off a bolted door, as if my cage is rattled. I am a grizzly waking from hibernation.

By the time Blackaby concludes, he is in tears.

"I've got to talk with this guy," I say.

"All right," Susie says. "I have to go find the children anyway."

Henry stands alone at the front of the altar. I wonder why people file out, why no one else wants to talk with the gentle man.

I stick out my hand and say, "Sir, my name is Jim. I've been a Christian since 1965, but I have a hardened heart. I'm a Vietnam vet."

He says, "I understand." Compassion seeps from him. He places his hand on my shoulder, and I feel myself relax.

He says, "Do you believe that God can take away your heart of stone and give you a heart of flesh?"

"Yes," I hear myself say.

"Then let's pray." Blackaby quotes a statement from Ezekiel, hundreds of years B.C.

"God," he prays, "take away Jim's heart of stone and give him a heart of flesh. Replace his heart with your heart."

Suddenly the floodgates open and fresh water streams into my soul. I close my eyes and watch the past being carried away on waves of forgiveness. Gone is the superficial concept of letting go, something I had struggled with for nearly thirty years. It is no longer just a concept, it is now a reality. I finally let go. And God filled me with love.

I look up and say, "He did it! He did it!"

I thank Blackaby with a hug, wiping tears from my eyes, and set off to find my wife.

I have finally found a way out of Vietnam.

Survivor's Guilt

Ed Foster sends an SOS, an e-mail. In it, I hear a cry for help. Every day for forty years he has awakened to the image of the dead Vietnamese boy. He was able to wipe it out by operating heavy equipment. Now that he's retired, he has time to think. Like a nail in a shoe, his pain is a constant reminder masked by his friendly smile.

Gary Bayles came home from Vietnam and hung up his 35mm Minolta in the back of the closet. The undeveloped roll of film sits in the camera today. We bury the hurt by hanging up the war.

Fred Silkey died from liver cancer in 2009. Captain Mayo died in 2004 from cancer.

Vito died in 2002 from liver disease. Ken Wiley survived thirteen major surgeries on his legs.

I recently met Mike who suffered the same plight as Ed. Mike witnessed a green troop accidentally shoot Lieutenant Lofthiem as he stood up. The chaos that followed is replayed now that Mike is retired.

Paul Nitzel tells me that the night Jimmy Burroughs was killed Doc Anderson sat down and cried so hard he couldn't be consoled. He had to be shipped out.

In October 2007, I attended a banquet with the men from the 4th/47th Infantry. Charlie Zies closed the night with a talk about Ronald "Chili" Saiz, describing the "worst day of my life, June 19, 1967." Charlie found consolation in his commitment to Christ.

The plaguing question arises: "Why did Chili die and not me?"

For me, pieces of my answer have been coming for years: a book, a touch, a chance meeting, a dream.

Then, one night not too long ago I rediscovered the 1949 Stanley Kramer film, *Home of the Brave*. In it, the main character Peter is a paralyzed victim of survivor's guilt. The doctor helps Peter to get past his problem and get on with life. He says, "Peter, every soldier in this world who sees his buddy get shot has that one moment when he feels glad. Yes, Peter, every single one of them, because deep down underneath he thinks, 'I'm glad it wasn't me. I'm glad I'm still alive.'"

When I heard those words on the screen, I knew I had found the missing piece of the puzzle.

The bottom line is this: *When someone is killed or injured, you're glad it wasn't you. You're glad you're still alive.* Survivor's guilt arises *after* the event, when the human mind has time to replay the traumatic scene.

I found total freedom when I accepted these truths.

I am glad that I am alive.

I am glad I wasn't killed.

Postscript

This is an excerpt from a letter I received from Chili's twin brother, Don Cuate, when I contacted him to tell him about the book and ask permission to publish Chili's pictures. Don was in the Navy. Chili's real name is Ronald. This is just as Don wrote it.

We left Viet Nam for the last time in end of December, 1966, headed for Japan, Hawaii then home. I would find out later that me and Ron would cross each other on the Pacific, according to his log.

One thing I want to say, I speak only of my time in the Navy and my experience in Viet Nam is just to let you all know just what I did, don't know if Ron really knew. I cannot in any way relate to what you all went thru. I can only say that If, you all know that big two letter word, "IF," Ron had not been drafted, but went into the Navy — well let me tell you, I don't think that way anymore, haven't for a long time.

I arrived back at the States, and we would continue to do exercises, after three days of being on my boat, we headed back to the Mother Ship. As we pulled up to the ship we were hoisted up onto the ship, unloaded our weapons and gear. I was told at that time that I had a call from home and they want me to call and ask for an operator and was given her number. After a while this got to be really confusing. I had a real bad feeling. Something was terribly wrong, and all I could think about was Ronald. As I proceed with trying to get in touch with someone I finally got in touch with my oldest brother from a payphone. He started to tell me about a friend of his,I tell you I was even more confused, if you knew this guy you would understand, what the heck he was trying to get to I didn't know I finally went back to the ship, as he asked me to do. Well, he said, Don I have to tell that Ronald was killed in Viet Nam, did not know how or when.

145

I said nothing. Just could not bring myself to think about anything. He asked if I was ok. I said yes. I really wasn't. He asked to speak to the XO officer. After a minute the XO asked if I wanted to wait until tomorrow. I said no, I wouldn't sleep anyway so he had the personnel officer to get me immediate leave.

I then went up to my bunk area, as I got there I put my fist into the first locker I saw and shouted out this f-----g war. One of my closest friends knew right away, and said it's Ronald isn't it. He held me for a minute, and asked if there was anything he could do for me.

One of my friends drove me to the Bus Depot. I had to fly out of Los Angeles the next morning. I was to fly on emergency leave, standby. There was no room for me. A man there overheard my situation, and said to the lady let him take my place. So I got to go home on that flight. He was Heaven sent.

As I sat at my seat waiting to take off I took the note out. Outside the window they were loading baggage. But this one guy was standing there. I just continued to look at him because all I could see was Ron standing there. I just stared at this person and all I could see was Ron just standing there. People say that the mind plays games on you especially at a time like this. I looked away and then looked back. He was gone.

Well I finally got home at midday, and was met at the airport by my brothers, I couldn't say anything at the moment. We just held each other and cried. On the trip home I asked, how did he die? They did not know at that time. That info came at a later time via the Army. I got home to see my parents and that was even harder for us, especially my mom. A little later went into our room we shared just to see it as it was before I left, the twin beds side by side. I just fell onto his bed and cried myself to sleep.

The days to follow we were met by people. Family and friends came by to express their condolences. I just wanted to leave there, to be alone, but I stuck it out. I don't actually recall just when I saw his girlfriend. I do know she was very broken hearted. I could see it in her especially at the services later. Virginia was her name. She stayed close to the family and was much a part of the proceedings to follow. To this day I share with her some of the things you all have sent me. I only wish she had been given a flag, also.

To go back a step we were told we could not see Ron's remains, My older brother got a hold of the Army officer in charge and said we wanted to see him, we did not want a misidentification. Our folks were not gonna bury the wrong soldier. So later it was authorized for the remains to be seen. I refused. My brothers only got to see him and were satisfied. The casket was then again sealed and not again opened for public viewing. I only wanted to remember him as I last saw him. That was in the picture I sent out to you all.

The funeral to follow was attended by so many people. Ron made many friends before he left school, and to find out later as well. He was buried in Fort Logan National Cementary. Sadly, we lost three other guys from school shortly after.

As time went on I eventually went back to the ship, only to deal with just wanting to get on and get out when my time was up. My folks and siblings wanted me to get out on hardship. This matter went on for quite some time. By the time it all got through, even though I really did not want out. It finally got to that point the captain ordered me to be processed out. I said no, I was to finish my tour. He cursed, and I stayed, and got out four months later.

I once again came home to the bedroom we once shared. I got back to being with friends and going out and working at this job where my dad retired from. I kept in touch with my brother's girlfriend and later we went our own ways. My life became a time of going out with friends on weekends mainly, at times weeknights. Each time I went out I just drank, at nights end, came home to the bedroom and looked over at the bed and just cried myself to sleep. Some nights when I didn't go out I couldn't sleep so I got up like at 4 a.m. and just sat in front of the church next door or went for long walks, at times for miles.

As I stated earlier I did not see my brother's remains, so I still in the back of my mind thought maybe, just maybe, he would still be alive regardless of what I heard or what was said. I wanted him to be with me again. Well, night after night of coming home drunk or sober I waited for him to come through that squeaky screen door we kept open on summer nights. On one night in particular I was sober I remember I said my nightly prayers. I again looked over at his bed just thought about us and our days prior to him leaving home. I turned over on my side, back to the door, and was about to go to sleep. I had this feeling of someone at my back. The house being the old house it was, the floors were creaky floors. Well after a minute or two I heard the floor start to creak. The sound approached my bed. As each step came closer toward me, I was too scared to turn around. I felt this hand on my shoulder. The hand just kind of tapped on it. It stopped, and I turned real quick. I saw no one. I just went to sleep after that.

The following morning I woke with this feeling of real peace, and I knew then that he was not coming home in physical form but had spiritually. And my days with him have been in that sense, spiritual. I did not again experience what I did that night. I feel I had some closure, in regards to thinking he may again come home to me as I had hoped he would.

My life certainly had its days in the years to come, its ups and downs. I would at times drink and sob, but it never really had ahold of me in most part. I quit drinking my favorite, Rum, in 1981. Quit smoking in 1987. Unfortunately other problems came up, like being with one woman. I think I was just too afraid to hold onto one, I might lose her also. I find it hard to really express love to anyone. Twice divorced, now married for 16 years. I am getting better about showing real love, and not just sexually.

I went through a lot of therapy over the years. One thing I was diagnosed with was PTSD, and I was homicidal. This matter became of much concern. I went through therapy for it for a long time. Some of the therapists I really did question. I just came to give it all to the Lord. Each day I start to feel down and some things come back. I just again pray more about it.

I am retired from the Transit Authority, now for three years. I tried a few full and part time jobs, but it all didn't work out. I just do side jobs carpentry, landscape, or odd stuff just try to keep busy and in shape w/ workouts. Foremost my life with my wife involves our being with our church. We are very active members of this church. It is a Christian Church close to home. I am closer to Jesus Christ now in past years than before. My faith is my strength. And knowing that Ron died with a Christian at his side, and shared the Word with him prior to his passing as you all have done, I have had a good feeling about that. I now know for sure he had the lord in his Heart, and is now in our Father's Kingdom with Jesus.

I hope this letter lets you all know more about me than before. You all don't know how much this means to me that you have gotten in touch with me. I have felt some closure, and as I write this I feel joy in my heart. Now I feel the strength from the Lord to love as I wanted to for years and to move forth with my Lord.

I certainly do feel blessed, again, to have you all there since you were a big part of Ron (Chili). Thanks ever so much. Hope someday we meet.

Blessings to you all and yours.

Till then,
Donald Cuate

Jim Marsh is a rare and good man who seeks to share his love and heart. What he writes is exemplified daily in his actions, attitude, and compassion for others. The real gift of what Jim Marsh writes is that he lives it out first.

—John R. Meyer, Lt Col, USAF Retired

There's always tomorrow, but not for everybody. I hope this book helps some.

—Fred Silkey, Vietnam Veteran

I hope Jim Marsh's book helps a lot of people who have PTSD.

—Bob Bayly, Vietnam Veteran

For additional information or to order, please visit
www.temenospublishing.com